Weave of Destiny

Ken Lefkowitz

Legacy Book Press LLC
Davenport, Iowa

Copyright © 2020 Ken Lefkowitz

Cover design by Madison Phillips

All rights reserved. No part of this book may be used or reproduced by any means, graphic, electronic, or mechanical, including photocopying, recording, taping or by any information storage retrieval system without the written permission of the publisher except in the case of brief quotations embodied in critical articles and reviews.

ISBN: 978-1-7347986-1-6
Library of Congress Control Number: 1-9043775991

DEDICATION

This book is dedicated to my wife, Sheila, whose diminutive stature and delicate charm belie her powerful courage within. Her smile brings the gift of warmth and kindness to most everyone she meets.

Sheila's strength of character and resiliency allowed both of us to move beyond traumatic and potentially devastating events to experiences that were both redemptive and life inspiring. From her, I learned the values of peace, love, and kindness in an appreciative embrace of life.

This is her story.

CONTENTS

CHAPTER 1 -- THE FIRST 1

CHAPTER 2 -- MOVING ON 11

CHAPTER 3 -- THE DECISION 19

CHAPTER 4 -- A CHANGE IN DIRECTION 39

CHAPTER 5 -- WAITING 57

CHAPTER 6 – THE PARK BENCH 65

CHAPTER 7 -- CONNECTICUT 73

CHAPTER 8 -- TWO WEEKS 87

CHAPTER 9 -- MOVING ON 101

CHAPTER 10 -- THE RETURN 113

CHAPTER 11 – EPILOGUE 127

ABOUT THE AUTHOR 129

CHAPTER 1 -- THE FIRST

"What was she like?" Sheila was in a hospital bed, her body propped up by a large pillow. "Tell me please."

"It doesn't matter."

"Please."

"It won't help to know."

"Please Ken, please."

Honoring each other's needs and requests was one of the foundations of our relationship. Her yearning for information was tugging at my gut, compelling me to speak.

"Well, ah, well," I stammered. "No, not that, ah, ah." The description I was thinking of stuck in my throat as I choked it back.

"I never saw her," Sheila sobbed mournfully, "and I need to know, I need a remembrance. Something. Can't you just tell me?"

"Well, oh well. Okay. I don't know how else to say it." Then I blurted out, "Deformed beyond recognition."

Sheila gasped.

"Well, not really that bad," I said, trying to soften my grisly description. I knew in my heart it was accurate, but awful. Her tiny body was dwarfed by the large hospital bed that seemed to engulf her. Rocked by the death of our baby and in great pain from her surgery, it took all of her emotional and physical strength not to break down.

Refusing to give in to overwhelming grief, she forced herself to rally from the depths of despair ripping at her consciousness, working to drag her deep into melancholy and depression. She dried her eyes, straightened her back, and raised her head.

"Oh, that's all right. You know I can take it," she responded in her usual stoic style, the expression of grudging acceptance written on her face. She was the strongest person I knew.

Sheila was taken aback, but not totally surprised by my terse and crude description of our baby. She had suspected that some aspect of deformity might be involved since she had carried with a huge distended belly and hadn't felt signs of life for a few weeks.

"Think of Carolyn as the baby that just wasn't meant to be," I exclaimed, trying to deflect Sheila's attention away from my description. "I know I will."

"I already have," Sheila said.

After knowing her for five years, I should have realized that she had moved beyond me in dealing with the death of our baby. Yes, she was forlorn. Yes, she was down, but not out. Not my wife.

I sat by the bed holding her arm that was punctured by a PICC line sending healing and protective fluids into her damaged body. She had carried our baby full-term, her belly expanded to unusual proportion by the fetus' large hydrocephalic cranium. Carolyn, the name we had given our baby before birth, had died in the womb late in Sheila's eighth month, killed by the seeping fluid accumulating in her brain. I was informed by Sheila's doctor that the baby was already dead but was sworn to withhold the information from her, so as not to upset her.

"She doesn't need to know. Sheila will find out soon, after we remove the baby by C-section," the doctor explained. "We need to do this because its head will rip her vaginal canal apart if we allow her to deliver naturally. Let her have some peace now."

"Okay," I responded, "if that's your professional advice."

It sure made it difficult for me when Sheila insisted that we stop at a few stores that sold baby clothing. Her face glowed with excitement as she peered into the store windows.

"Aren't those outfits cute? Let's go in and buy one or two."

It was all I could do to smile and not cry, the truth concealed as the doctor had instructed.

To this day, I look back and question whether that was the right decision. It seemed to me to be callous, or even cruel, to deceive my wife in this way, knowing that her happiness was only temporary. But in those days, a doctor's advice was not to be questioned. And I was a young man, still not sure of myself and wondering about life in general. So, I accepted a medical professional's directions even though all of my instincts told me they violated my relationship with my wife. I rationalized that by staying true to the doctor's strategy, I was somehow protecting her, but I was torn apart inside.

*****

In Sheila's eighth month when I had returned home, I was still dressed in my fatigues and combat boots. The war in Vietnam was raging some months after American forces had reclaimed much of the territory lost to the Viet Cong and North Vietnamese Regulars during the Tet Offensive of 1968. When I completed basic training at Fort Jackson in South Carolina, with a heavy dose of jungle combat skills, I was assigned to advanced artillery training on 105 and 155 Howitzers at Fort Sill, Oklahoma.

"We're all headed to Nam," George explained in a muffled voice as if he were revealing a grand state secret.

"Those of us in selected batteries will be assigned to airborne artillery. We'll be dropped out of Huey choppers behind the DMZ with our pieces and then set up our cannons. Our assignment will be to keep the roads across the DMZ free of North Vietnamese troops moving over the border to South Vietnam."

"I know a guy who was in the first unit to go in. His chopper ride over the DMZ went smoothly. When they reached just over the border, they hovered so they could deliver their payload. Canon sections were dropped to the ground easily. The troops to follow would assemble them and set them to try to protect the DMZ from enemy crossings.

"When the soldiers began climbing down rope ladders, all hell broke loose. Rifle fire and mortars turned the air into a death trap. In a few minutes, many were dead or wounded. Most were hit by enemy fire. Others were badly injured after being blown off the rope ladders by explosions. He said the carnage was unbelievable. The chopper was splattered with blood. A few soldiers, even though injured like him, made it to the woods. Most either died or were captured. Many of the more seriously wounded were executed where they lay on the ground. More than half of the choppers didn't make it back. The unit took an estimated seventy percent casualties. That was no ordinary firefight; it was a massacre, a suicide mission.

"We had better prepare ourselves for heavy fighting. What you just heard is what we're going to face, none of it good. It could be death, crippling injury, or some North Vietnamese nightmare like a POW camp."

George finished his prediction with the same covert tone as it began. We had no way of determining whether George's friend's description was accurate or just an unsubstantiated inflated story. We didn't know if George's assurance that we were next was simply a rumor. Still, it continued to be echoed by others in the barracks. And barracks' rumors somehow seem to have proven accurate.

Two weeks later, our CO informed us we were going to 'Nam. During the next few days of heavy training, we were haunted by the images of George's story while contemplating some horrible fate or certain death. Few of us slept, staying up all night in order to maximize our time before we were sent on our own suicide mission. After my unit was deployed to Southeast Asia, I was summoned by my Battalion Commander, accompanied by a Red Cross representative who handed me an airline ticket and said, "This is your ticket back home. We provide this service for those soldiers who are unable to afford travel for emergencies." He handed me an airline ticket to New York.

I found out later that Sheila's psychiatrist told her, "Now that I have been seeing you for a time, I'm going to craft a strong letter to Ken's commanding officer to have him returned home. As your psychiatrist, I'm concerned about your emotional health, especially in light of your pregnancy and your husband's absence. Your uncle had suggested this to me when you started seeing me at his urging. I'll prepare the letter and send it out this afternoon."

After agreeing softly as the psychiatrist assured her she'd move quickly, Sheila left the office not knowing what to think, but she was filled with the hope that she might be seeing me again soon.

A short time passed, and it became evident the psychiatrist's letter had a powerful impact. I was reassigned to a new post only a half-hour drive from our modest apartment in Brooklyn.

"Reporting for duty sir." I delivered the words crisply, standing tall at attention.

"At ease, soldier," the receiving officer at Fort Wadsworth in Staten Island, New York, barked as I handed him my papers.

"You're assigned here at Fort Wadsworth on a Compassionate Reassignment, as ordered by your CO."

This transfer had happened just at the time Sheila began to question why she no longer felt movement and kicking in her distended abdomen.

******

Still standing at Sheila's hospital bedside, my focus returned to the present. She shifted in some pain while she squeezed my hand, looking deeply into my eyes and said, "Our baby died, but at least you're alive."

Pausing for a moment, she concluded reflectively, "Maybe Carolyn died so you could live."

My thoughts were conflicted at hearing my wife's words. Nevertheless, trade-off or not, even facing the grim circumstances in front of us, I was certainly pleased to be by her side and not fighting in Vietnam. It was a war that many considered unjust, even illegal, that was trying the patience of the American public. I felt somewhat guilty that other boys and former comrades were giving their lives for a political travesty. I was in uniform but not fighting for what I had been trained to do. Yet, I was happy to avoid the full-year assignment in Vietnam.

The day passed slowly for both of us. Sheila's incision, extending from her navel to her groin, was raw and sensitive. The medication dripping through her PICC line provided some relief.

"Oooh," she moaned softly as she shifted her position in bed. Wincing in pain with every movement of her body, Sheila tried to remain still.

"Here, let me wipe your forehead with some cool water."

Her discomfort and her loss seemed to be somewhat eased by my attention as I dabbed her brow and back of her neck with a towel dipped in ice water.

"Oh, that feels great. It's so soothing. Thanks."

We held hands for hours while the sun slowly set in the dreary Brooklyn sky. As the evening arrived, ushering in the hospital's visiting hours, friends and close family began to visit. They gathered in all the open spaces of Sheila's room.

"So sorry for your loss. Are you feeling okay after the surgery?"

One by one, they approached her to offer both vocal and physical expressions of sympathy. Many kissed her or held her hand. Her kindness and warm personality attracted people to her. Everyone loved her deeply and hurt for her. Most shed tears and some sobbed as they whispered by her bedside.

It was most comforting for Sheila that so many people who touched her in countless ways had come to provide support when she most needed them. She took nothing for granted in her life.

At first, the room was quiet, solemn. Only words expressed in hushed tones could be heard. Slowly the talk increased to more audible levels. After a while, some chuckling and subdued laughter broke out as the visitors took their cue from Sheila to lighten the mood. Joining in, they tried to be cheery and help. Sheila brightened everyone's spirits. For many people in her condition, this may have seemed inappropriate. But these were not just acquaintances, they knew Sheila well and all were aware of her stalwart personality and strength of character. Complaining or embracing a lingering sense of remorse was out of the question. No pity would be accepted openly. The joy of life would be the essential element of Sheila's recovery, as it was for her everyday existence.

"Oh, that pulls on my incision. It hurts a bit." The words passed through Sheila's lips even as they still turned up in a smile.

"I'd better be a little more careful," she said reluctantly, transforming her laugh into a soft chuckle.

As the lighthearted chatter continued, Sheila's physical pain and aching loss faded from her visitors' consciousnesses.

"What a gentle smile, and those beautiful sparkling eyes. And she can even laugh through her pain," I heard one friend say to another admiringly.

"What else would you expect from Sheila?" was the reply.

The atmosphere in the room quickly turned to a mild, soothing merriment. The gathering celebrated Sheila's embrace of life they all had experienced through the years.

"It's hard to believe this is the hospital room of a post-surgical mother who lost her baby only the day before. Sheila's amazing. I always knew that she's a terrific person."

Words of praise, relaxed conversations, and light laughter filled the air.

Suddenly the mood changed. Sheila's mother, Rose, arrived, displaying her usual glum expression. She had not been with her daughter during the ordeal and had not come to her side the first day of the tragic event.

Rose entered the room in her customary labored slow walk, her shoulders rounded, head down. She stopped three feet from the end of Sheila's bed where the doctor's and nurse's charts dangled from the post. Not progressing any further toward her daughter, avoiding touching her or demonstrating any degree of caring, Rose raised her head pathetically and with great annoyance.

"You have no idea how difficult it was for me to get here. I had to pick up my vitamins after work, then take a bus and a train to get to this hospital." The air in the room thickened.

"I'm very tired," she continued, breathing a sigh of exhaustion. "Now I have to take even a longer trip home."

Immediately after Rose's report, the mood in the room shifted dramatically, the buoyant uplifting vibrations shattered. The lightness sucked out by her words.

First a hush, then an uncomfortable silence pervaded the air as the visitors stood stunned in slack-jawed amazement. No one could believe what they had just witnessed.

"Well, I guess I'll go home now," Rose uttered in a hardly audible voice full of self-pity.

After demonstrating her usual self-centered callousness toward her daughter, she turned and slowly shuffled out of the room. Her head was down, her normal sourness painted on her face. She left without the slightest expression of compassion for Sheila, only raising her shoulders while breathing in, and then exhaling a breath of disgust.

In the moment, I hurt terribly for Sheila, hoping she would receive some support from her mother. But I had experienced Rose before, ever cold and harshly judgmental, incapable of kindness and caring, even for someone as wonderful as my wife, her own child. So nothing that had just transpired surprised me.

Within minutes of Rose's departure, the rest of the visitors began leaving, still amazed at what they had seen and heard.

"Goodbye. Be well."

"Take care. We'll see you soon."

"Again, so sorry for your loss. Bye."

Sheila and I were left alone, comforting each other's grief.

Later, after I'd returned home, I got a call from my mother.

"Grandma had a stroke. She's in the hospital unconscious," she explained, agitated and harried. I hung up the phone and rushed out of the apartment, hurrying to my wife's bedside.

Sheila was very close with my grandmother. The two were quite similar: small of stature, always friendly, and giving to anyone they meet. Both were warm and sincere. Amiable, ebullient, together they were a duo of kindness and caring; they were loved by most everyone.

Sheila smiled when I arrived. But her expression changed quickly when I shared the news.

"My grandma's in another hospital with a stroke."

"What?" she said softly in disbelief.

Neither of us spoke for a few minutes. We looked at each other, squeezing the other's hand. We were numbed by the second shock in our lives in just forty-eight hours.

"When I leave, I'll go visit her." I broke the silence with a mundane empty statement. It was all I could think to say.

"Oh, I'd love to see her too," Sheila said, her eyes watery and swollen. "Squeeze her hand and give her a kiss from me." Then she turned quiet again.

"I'm sure that losing the baby had something to do with it. Grandma was so excited for us. Carolyn's death must have been too much for her to bear," she said and then fell silent again for a few moments. She was pensive and pained. "Oh, I feel so guilty. So guilty."

"Please love," I pleaded. "You can't blame yourself. Don't blame yourself. All of this was out of your control." I nudged her leg. "C'mon. Smile. Please let me see your beautiful smile."

"It's hard. So hard. Grandma, you know."

"Sure I do. But you just can't feel guilty about this. It's not your fault. Not at all."

"Oh, but the baby. Grandma was so happy for us. How she must have been devastated. And then the stroke."

"Please, stop blaming yourself."

"How I would love to leave this bed and go see her."

"You can't babe. You need to focus on your own recovery."

"And anyway, from what Mom told me, Grandma isn't aware of anything. She's in a coma."

Sheila didn't respond. She was now openly sobbing.

"Well, at least when you see her later, when you kiss her cheek for me, tell her, 'I'm sorry.' So very sorry."

"I will. And if it comes from you, she might even hear me, coma and all."

Tears came more heavily down Sheila's face.

"I love you, Ken."

"I love you too," I responded.

"Look, I know this news about Grandma has thrown you for a loop. Just don't let it set you back."

"I can't help it."

"Okay. You look tired. It would be good if you rested. Try to sleep. Here's some water first."

I let Sheila drink some ice water through a straw, her lips still parched after her surgery. Then as she closed her eyes and her breathing became heavy, I slipped out of the room to go see my grandmother.

A gnawing feeling of having made a huge mistake telling Sheila about Grandma was eating at me. I was ashamed of myself. All I wanted to do was to help Sheila mend, soothe her, ease her loss. Instead, I upset her with news that perhaps could have waited, for a while anyway. I had selfishly shared my own distress about my grandmother without thinking of the effect it would have on my wife. But our relationship centered on openness with each other, and I had simply followed that path.

Never gaining consciousness, four days later, my grandmother passed away.

CHAPTER 2 -- MOVING ON

A few months after Carolyn died, Sheila's incision had mostly healed, and she had nearly reclaimed her customary life. Soon she would be returning to her profession as a dental hygienist.

"It's nice to be back to a normal life," she told her friend Marilyn. They had met at a New York City Department of Health dental clinic where they both were employed. Together with Louise, Sheila's other close friend, Marilyn was a comfort for both of us.

"Thanks so much for just being there for us. It's truly wonderful to have friends like you." I expressed my gratitude awkwardly since verbalizing feelings and emotions was not one of my strong suits. "I really appreciate you going to our apartment and removing all the baby stuff we bought. It really made it a lot easier when Sheila came home from the hospital. It sure spared me from a task I wasn't looking forward to. Thanks."

"That's what good friends do." Marilyn and Louise smiled at me in response.

*****

"Given what you just went through, I'm submitting your name to be considered for an Honorable Hardship Discharge," the

Colonel and Commandant of Fort Wadsworth explained to me in a very official, but sympathetic voice. "Of course, the letter from your wife's psychiatrist to the Hardship Review Committee held some sway in the decision."

I was aware of the influence Sheila's uncle had in this process. He had asked his friend, the psychiatrist, to write the letter explaining that Sheila's situation required my presence. Also, I was quite grateful to Sheila's sister who had loaned her some money to pay the psychiatrist's bills. Little if anything could be afforded on a soldier's paltry pay in the late 1960s.

"I also want to offer my appreciation for good performance," the Colonel added. "You worked quite hard and delivered on all the tasks I assigned you. Many of these required sound judgment and mature discretion."

After I received my Honorable Discharge papers in the mail, Sheila was relieved. "Our baby may have died. But you weren't part of your unit that took so many casualties in Vietnam. Not fighting in that unjust political war. The government can't ask you to serve again. They can't draft you anymore. You're alive and home. And now you're free."

We both had voted for Lyndon Johnson in the 1964 presidential election against Barry Goldwater, whose policies included escalating the war in Vietnam, threatening to deploy nuclear weapons if required.

"Better dead than red" was the approach Goldwater advocated, which linked to the "Domino Theory." This referred to the desire of the Soviet Union and China's alleged objective of spreading their Communist ideology around the world, by force if necessary. Under the doctrine, the goal of the United States was to prevent the growth of Communism, providing a distorted reason for the war.

Unfortunately, President Johnson, who opposed this approach, actually escalated the war, drafting tens of thousands of young men, many of whom were against the war and Goldwater.

"Hey, hey LBJ, how many boys did you kill today?" demonstrators chanted outside of the White House.

They felt that President Johnson had betrayed them, fighting a war based on flawed principles and one that was patently unfair to the Vietnamese people. Both the populations of the North and South were suffering terribly and should have been allowed the freedom to determine their own form of government. Within these conditions, the U.S. military was drafting many young men. Yet it had seen fit to let me go.

Neither Sheila nor I could know that fourteen years later we would be visiting the Vietnam Memorial in Washington. Sheila would be holding me as my hands covered my bowed head and I wept uncontrollably. Already having discovered ten names on the long black wall, I stopped counting, for these were more than just letters etched in stone. They were reminders of vibrant young men I had known and served with taken before their time. I could hear their voices and see their bright faces.

Over the next few months, I began the process of finding a job. I filled my days responding to classified advertisements, while personally visiting companies and search firms in Manhattan. Gathering a wealth of career information, I scored well on numerous aptitude tests administered by hiring organizations who offered me positions from Junior Programmer to Credit Rater Trainee to Junior Market Research Analyst.

"We are pleased to offer you the position of Personnel Research Analyst," the recruiter for a major pharmaceutical company said graciously. I really wasn't certain what this job entailed, but it offered almost 20% more compensation than the other positions.

"They offered me nearly nine thousand dollars a year," I told Sheila when I returned home from the final interview. That was a fine starting salary in 1969.

"That's great. Now that I'm back working as a hygienist, between the two of us we'll have enough money to start buying some things we always wanted. A decent apartment, some living room furniture, a bedroom set. We might even be able to save up some money."

We were in the best economic situation we had ever experienced. Both of us had grown up in poor homes. Our current earnings situation created exciting prospects for the future.

*****

"Wow, this bedroom furniture is beautiful, the dresser, the bureau, the headboard. Who would have ever thought we could afford things this lovely?"

Sheila was beaming with excitement as the delivery men placed the furniture where she had directed them along our bedroom walls. We were reveling in our solid financial situation and its resulting newfound comfort.

Yet, our hearts longed for a child. We both yearned for a baby at the same time we experienced lingering grief over the loss of our first. Although at times our minds could escape this childless reality, frequently the empty hollowness returned, especially during quiet times. Still, true to a personality trait we both shared, but most pronounced in Sheila, we quickly began to focus on the future.

"Will this loss affect our ability to have the four kids we always talked about? Will we be able to have biological children, a footprint of our own for the future? How do we move forward?" we wondered together.

"Your baby's condition is called hydrocephalus, which means having excess fluid on the brain," our doctor had explained. "If she had lived, major issues, both mental and physical, would have plagued her. Even then, she may not have survived for more than a few years.

"I know that both of you are extremely disappointed, crestfallen at your tragedy. But you were spared the very real burden of a severely disabled child whose life would have been a struggle at best. I've seen fetal survival under these conditions rip a marriage apart and leave the pieces on the ground."

"Thanks for the perspective, Doctor," I said, expressing my appreciation for a straight, no-nonsense piece of valuable information. But now we need to move forward."

"Please tell us the cause of our baby's deformity. Did we pass her death on to her through our genes?" Sheila asked.

"This condition doesn't necessarily run in families, so it may not be genetic. It may have been a lack of folic acid or some other issue. We just don't know. But certainly, you should consider genetic counseling to help you to decide your future family status."

"Thanks so much for your guidance," Sheila said when we left the office as the doctor walked us to the door, his arm around my shoulder.

"Goodbye, and good luck," he said, leaving us to find our own way.

"Our tests indicate no sign of genetic issues," the specialist told us, a physician who was recommended by a friend. "I see no indication of attribution here.

"I believe that you, unfortunately, experienced the one in ten thousand births that involve some form of spinal or brain problems. Please recognize, however, that we cannot be certain. The odds may point in one direction, reality in another.

"Good luck to you in the future."

We drove away from the meeting in a confused fog. Neither of us spoke. Discordant thoughts deeply troubled us both.

"Where do we go from here?" Sheila asked.

"It looks good for more kids, but not certain. Could we hit the long odds again, even if nothing is wrong with either one of us?"

"I'm thinking the same thing," I responded somberly.

"We could be asking why us, but what good would that do? Taking a chance is scary, especially if it means another C-section for you."

"Yeah, the OB-GYN told me once a C-section like the one I had is performed, normal delivery is out of the question. Another one could rupture the incision even if it's healed." Sheila stated clearly what I already knew.

"Maybe we should call Gary and ask his advice."

"Great idea," Sheila agreed.

Later, the phone rang. I picked it up quickly. It was our friend, Gary, a practicing physician in California, returning my call.

"Are you guys okay?" Gary asked. "When I heard that you called, I was hoping that everything was alright with you two."

"We're fine, Gary," I responded. "We've been trying to pick up the pieces over the last few months, and I think that we're hurting a lot less. Of course, close friends like you and family have helped. We are really focusing on the future now."

"I'm glad to hear that. Picking up the pieces is difficult. I tend to forget that your grandmother died right after your baby. It really was a tough time for you. But focusing on moving forward is good for you guys. Great!"

"That brings us to the purpose of our phone call, aside from hearing a good friend's voice that is. Actually, we're looking for some guidance."

"Okay, shoot"

"Gary, as you know, we have gone for genetic counseling. And although no ascertainable genetic issues were detected, they cannot be ruled out. That's a mixed message for us. We sure still want to have our own biological children, but we're not looking for a repeat of what we just went through."

"Of course you're not." I heard on the other side of the phone.

"So, we're seeking your advice as a doctor and a friend who's known us for a long time. Do you have an opinion about what we should do? Should we adopt a child or try again to get pregnant?"

A brief silence ensued.

"You sure may want to consider adopting. But if you think that a decade or so in the future you will regret not trying again to have your own biological child, you may want to think about another pregnancy now. Of course, both paths are not mutually exclusive."

"Wow, am I glad we called you. We've been rolling our

options over and over in our minds. You've given us a new and very reasonable perspective."

"Glad I could help. But please remember, I'm not you. Follow your heart. Let your spirit guide you. I'm just a physician, not an oracle."

"Having known you for so many years, I knew you would conclude with that last remark. We trust you and value your opinion more than anyone else we know. So thanks again. You've given us a lot to think about."

"No problem at all. I'm here if you need me," Gary offered. "Call anytime. And good luck with your decision. Just remember, be true to yourselves. Listen to your feelings."

CHAPTER 3 -- THE DECISION

Sheila and I weighed our alternatives, our feelings, and Gary's advice nearly every day over a few months. Then----.

"Decision made," said Sheila. "At least I think so this time. Right?"

"Yep, you and I are going to try again. This time, I know will be a success," I declared, displaying my most optimistic thoughts, as much as I could summon. Still, doubts and a modest amount of fear colored our expectations. The smiles on our faces belied a tense anxiety filling our dreams.

We cleared Sheila's health status with her doctor. The only reservation was that she would need another C-section. This was required to avoid harm after the first procedure weakened her uterus wall. Sheila was okay with it, so I felt comfortable with our decision.

"You're pregnant again." Sheila's doctor relayed his diagnosis.

She had missed her second menstrual cycle and was fairly certain another life was forming within her before her visit to the doctor. The doctor simply confirmed what she already suspected.

From then on things progressed quite smoothly.

"Wow, I can see I'm carrying much smaller than last time."

Friends and family had remarked during her first pregnancy that Sheila was carrying what seemed to be unusually large and low. Shy of five feet tall and only about ninety pounds, she was quite petite. Her size was seen as the predictor of her condition. It was only in her very late-term that the doctor had begun to believe that something was wrong.

"I'm feeling great. This time I feel really active life. Strong active life," Sheila said as I held my hands on her belly.

"I can feel the rolling of limbs and jerking kicks." I responded to the movement in Sheila's stomach. We were happy with the doctor's encouraging words supporting our experience.

"Isn't it wonderful? What a warm and gentle feeling I have all over. I feel like I'm already bonding with this baby."

A few joyful, yet anxious, months passed. Sheila was carrying much smaller than last time. The doctor continued his optimism, nearly certain that this second fetus was free of the affliction that had doomed the first.

"I feel fine. And the baby is so very active," Sheila told him.

"Great," the doctor responded. "We'll schedule you for a C-section a week from today. I'm sure that everything will go well this time. All the markers that we have the capability of checking on look good."

"The nurse will call you in a day or two to let you know when to check in to the hospital."

"Thanks," Sheila said as we left the doctor's office.

"I love you," we pledged to each other, feeling some relief from the long months of waiting.

Holding hands and smiling, we walked to our car and drove home. We were anxious, but a sanguine feeling filled us both.

*****

"It's taking a long time," I said to my brother, Mark. A concerned expression grew on my face.

We were in the waiting room. I had begged to be part of the

birth process by observing the C-section in the operating room. But the medical protocols of the day denied me access.

"Don't worry. It'll be fine."

Just as Mark finished his reassurance, the doctor entered the waiting room, wrapped in his scrubs.

"Congratulations! You have a son."

Holding his hand out, he smiled warmly as I grabbed his outstretched palm and shook it heartily. Up and down, up and down, almost fiercely.

"Okay, okay. I know that you're happy, but I need my hand for the other procedures I have scheduled for today. Don't end my career," the doctor joked as I shook his whole body.

A broad smile covered my face, my eyes tearing with unimagined joy.

"A nurse will come get you when Sheila wakes from anesthesia. I know you want to see her and your newborn son." Then the doctor left.

I sat quietly for a while, happy thoughts flooding my mind.

"What a great day." The words passed my lips, directed at no one in particular.

"Yep," was all I heard from my younger brother; a teenager not yet comfortable with expressing his emotions. I knew that he was beaming inside since Mark was hurt badly by our first loss.

After a while, a young woman dressed in white came to get me. She led me to the nursery where I laid eyes on my son for the first time.

"Wow, what a sight," was all I could say as she pointed to our baby.

"Your wife is in room 308. Just wait about fifteen minutes, and then you can go see her," I heard the young woman say.

I stood at the nursery window full of delight.

"Your kid likes to kick his legs," said a father who was standing next to me, admiring his own newborn.

I smiled at these words, savoring the idea of being a father.

About twenty minutes passed. As much as I wanted to see Sheila, I was having trouble tearing myself away from the nursery. But then the desire to share this wonderful sight with her overcame me. I walked quickly to room 308, feeling as though I was floating through the hospital corridor.

Still in pain from her surgery and groggy from the anesthesia, Sheila managed a smile as I entered the room. A nurse walked by as I came closer to her bed.

"And how are you?" she said to the woman in the next bed to Sheila. All new mothers shared a semi-private room in this hospital.

I stopped at Sheila's side; her gnawing pain was expressed on her face. I lightly pushed aside the PICC line dripping into her right arm and gently clasped her hand.

"How is he?" she murmured.

"He's just wonderful. I just saw him in the nursery."

"The doctor told me that it will be a day or so until they can bring him to me. My incision needs to heal a bit before they will risk it. I can't wait. What a glorious thing it will be to hold him close. I'm wild with love for him, and I haven't even seen him. I'm just so happy."

"Of course you are."

"Ken, I'd like some ice water. I'm hot and thirsty."

I poured some water and ice in a cup. Before I raised it to her lips, I wiped her brow with a wet towel.

"That's so nice. I love you. What a great moment in our lives."

"I love you too," I answered.

Sheila's eyelids grew heavy.

"I'm so tired," she sighed. "So tired and so very happy."

With that, she closed her eyes.

I pulled up a chair and held Sheila's hand. Her torso rose and fell slowly while she drifted off into a deep sleep.

Spending that afternoon calling relatives and friends, I

informed them of the good news. Periodically I grew dizzy with excitement as I told everyone about our new son.

"Well, Gary, it's a boy. I'm a dad." I bugled at Gary on the phone.

"Great news. Congratulations, Dad." His voice was full of warm wishes. "Give Sheila a kiss for me. Now go enjoy your new son."

I even stopped at a store and proudly purchased a box of cigars. Each smoke was wrapped in cellophane reading, "It's a Boy." I felt on top of the world as I exited the store with a broad smile on my face. I headed to the hospital floating down the sidewalk.

That evening, Sheila's room was full of visitors beaming with the good news.

"Congratulations to both of you."

"He's so cute. Kicks like a champ."

"You two deserve this happiness."

"We're so happy for the both of you."

The cheery crowd was all smiles. Except for my mother, who pulled me aside and whispered, "He looks healthy enough. But he's so thin, and I think he's breathing heavily. But what do I know? It's the doctors that count." Then her arm was grabbed by one of the well-wishers, and she spun around to join the celebration in the room. With all the excitement, I was on a high and soon forgot my mother's words.

That night, when quiet returned after visiting hours were over, Sheila decided we should complete our baby naming papers.

"Matthew," she declared. "What a glorious name."

"Matthew it is," I agreed, bursting with pride.

*****

The phone rang at about six the next morning.

"This is Nurse Walters. Please come to the hospital as soon as you can. Your baby is very sick."

I threw on some clothes and hurried to the hospital. Before I raced off, I called my parents' house to let them know the situation.

"Dad is already on the subway going to work. I'll get in the car with Mark and we'll be there soon to help any way we can," my mother offered after a few moments of shocked silence.

I knew she was shattered by the news. Not only was her infant grandchild ill, but she was also crushed for Sheila and me. My mother and Sheila were very close. They would talk many times a week, and she loved her like the daughter she never had.

"Your son is quite ill. His lungs are not functioning properly. We're not equipped to handle his issues here, so we've ordered an ambulance to take him to a major regional hospital with an infant intensive care unit that should be able to address your son's problems. They're the best in the area."

The staff pediatrician's voice sounded like he was miles away. My head was spinning so fast I could barely understand his words. I felt as if I was in a tunnel and his explanation was echoing off the walls. I was rocked to the core and staggered by this change.

"I need to see my wife," was all I could say.

"You can ride in the ambulance to the hospital and attend to your son," was his response. "But you need to rush downstairs to the emergency area right now. Otherwise, you'll miss them before they leave. I'll inform your wife for you."

Not thinking clearly, I followed the doctor's directions blindly, rushing downstairs to catch the ambulance.

"We'll follow behind in our car in case you need us," my mother said, trying to take some helpful action. She and my brother, Mark, had arrived only about ten minutes after me.

"Get in the front seat," shouted the driver as I arrived at the ambulance bay. "A nurse is in the back with your son. Get in. There's no time to lose."

Just as I jumped in, barely seated, the ambulance lurched forward, achieving breakneck speed in less than a minute. Sirens blasting, lights glaring, it screamed through the city streets, running red lights and stop signs. The poorly maintained pot-holed streets of

Brooklyn seemed to reach out, intending to snarl our ride.

I was jolted from shoulder to shoulder, tossed from side to side within the cab. Our glaring lights reflected off the buildings lining the streets. Horns honked nervously as a few cars nearly collided with the racing vehicle.

"Hang on!" the driver yelled as we blazed our way through Brooklyn's thoroughfares. I hardly noticed the chaos, my mind focused on our son.

After an incredible ride that tested all of the driver's skills, the ambulance arrived at the new hospital's emergency area. The rear doors flung open and a stretcher was hoisted and then lowered to a waiting attendant, the accompanying nurse close behind. I bolted out of the front cab, trying to follow, but I was intercepted just beyond the doors.

"Stay here in the waiting area," a nurse instructed me as she blocked my path. "Slow down. Try to relax. I know that you're excited. But please have a seat in the emergency room arrival area. We'll call you up as soon as your baby is settled. We received a phone call from the pediatrician of your other hospital, so we're prepared for your son".

"What? Wait. Hold it. I want to see him."

"Okay. You will, just not right now when we need to deal with his immediate needs. You'll only be in the way, and our experience is that it's best parents don't see their baby until stabilized. Then you can see him. And you can talk with Dr. Rice who will be caring for him in the Infant Intensive Care Unit."

She grabbed me firmly by the shoulders and directed me to a seat. The nurse had to shove me gently backwards into the comfortable chair.

"Just try to relax until we come and get you."

I was agitated beyond my own control. Shaken and confused, I leaned my head backward, resting it on the top rear of my chair. I took a few deep breaths attempting to calm down. It was useless.

After a short while, which seemed like an eternity, a different nurse approached me. She repeated my name several times before she decided to touch my arm in order to get my attention. So many horrible thoughts were swirling around in my mind, I could hardly hear her.

"We're ready to take your son to the Infant Intensive Care Unit upstairs. The doctor will see you there. Time is critical so let's go. We need to hurry."

Just then, Mark and my mother ran into the emergency room waiting area from the parking lot. They heard what the nurse had told me as they entered the area.

"Go with Ken. I'll wait here," my mother instructed Mark. "Let me know what's happening as soon as you find out."

Matthew was now strapped to an emergency room gurney. He was attached to so many medical devices and tubes it was hard to see his little body around them. We were all sickened by the gruesome scene.

A lead attendant and the nurse behind the stretcher hurried through a pair of doors, Mark and I following close behind. They wheeled the bed as fast as they safely dared through a maze of hospital corridors. We could barely keep up.

"The elevator bank is just ahead," the nurse instructed the attendant in front. No elevator was available because they were servicing other floors.

"Since we're so pressed for time, I'll use my key." She inserted a key into a slot at the side of the elevator bank. Within a minute an elevator arrived. The doors opened. The bed was carefully, yet swiftly, guided into the rectangular box.

"Get in. Get in," the nurse barked at Mark and me trailing behind the bed.

We rode to the fourth floor.

Exiting the elevator, the bed was spun to the right. Mark and I followed down a long hall and then through a few short corridors.

"Damn, damn." The nurse cursed loudly as she realized that

we were on the wrong floor. "Those damned keys took us to the wrong floor!"

We whipped around immediately. Backtracking to the elevator at warp speed, we got in and rode to the correct floor. Following a sign clearly pointing to the Infant Intensive Care Unit, we flew down the hall. I was scarcely aware of my surroundings as I proceeded on like a frenetic robot.

"Stop and wait here," the nurse commanded. She, the attendant, and my son disappeared through two doors.

Mark and I waited where we were told, catching our breaths as we stood nervously in the hallway. We were anxious to understand Matthew's condition and what the medical staff was doing to help him.

"I'm Dr. Rice, and you are the father I assume." A tall, handsome man in a white lab coat extended his hand in a greeting. He had entered by the same doors through which Matthew's bed had been taken.

"Hi," was all I could say, hoping that he would continue on without my asking questions.

"Please stay here," he addressed Mark.

The doctor then guided me through the doors to the Infant Intensive Care Unit and to a crib partially covered by a plastic dome. Matthew's tiny body was heaving up and down as he labored for his breath. His head was barely visible; it was covered by numerous tubes that reached into his mouth and nose. A machine was helping him breathe.

"Go ahead. You can touch him if you want," the doctor offered, an expression of great concern on his face.

I reached under the plastic dome and gently touched my son's hand. His fingers and palm were so small that they disappeared from view within my grasp. His arm was trembling as I held him, and I noticed that his legs were too. I could see his heart throbbing in his chest as he panted desperately.

"Your baby has hyaline membrane disease, or HMD for

short, otherwise known as respiratory distress syndrome."

I tried to listen intently to Dr. Rice. Just observing Matthew's tormented suffering, I knew that he was in dire jeopardy.

"I won't take you through all the medical jargon, but I'll give it to you straight. You can see that your son is struggling mightily to breathe. Perhaps beyond his ability as time moves forward. His alveoli, or air sacs, are collapsing and he is being challenged to take in oxygen. Carbon dioxide is accumulating rapidly in his blood, leading to a condition called acidosis, which damages other organs in his body. We continue to test his blood to ascertain the degree of this breakdown. Unfortunately, it is deteriorating."

I didn't react for a few moments when the doctor paused. Then I gathered myself as best that I could.

"So what can you do to help him?" I asked, knowing that given the explanation I heard and observing my son's condition, the response wouldn't be positive or optimistic.

"Well, we are doing all we can. As you can see, we're trying to help him breathe. Also, we are giving him medicine that is designed to help his lungs. Unfortunately, your son is a very troubled baby."

Dr. Rice's calm and clinical demeanor suddenly changed. He became disturbed and agitated.

"The pediatrician from the hospital in which your son was born called here to let us know that he was sending your baby to our care. I don't understand what took him so long. Judging by his current condition, this infant has been declining rapidly for quite some time—many hours, I suspect. In these cases, time is of the essence."

Dr. Rice was growing quite angry, raising his voice.

"Now that his condition has degenerated to the state he's in, all of the actions we're taking may have no effect. The key is to treat HMD immediately, or very shortly after birth. Your son could have been helped if he had arrived here much sooner than he did. I can't understand for the life of me why he wasn't transported here last night, or even sooner. What took them so long? These symptoms don't come on in minutes; they become more pronounced and physically noticeable over hours. Didn't they observe his breathing in the nursery? Didn't they test his blood? Are they aware of the signs for potential illness in babies? What kind of training and experience with infants do they have?"

Two nurses attending babies in nearby cribs couldn't help but hear Dr. Rice's words. They turned toward us with looks of surprise.

His rhetorical questions received no answers when he stopped abruptly. Catching himself, Dr. Rice must have recognized that he was, in essence, questioning another doctor's skill and another facility's competency. In fact, Dr. Rice's tone was beyond questioning, it was derogatory. His disparaging remarks, although factually accurate, seemed unprofessional and appeared to represent the basis for a medical malpractice lawsuit.

"Well, um, oh… But you see these types of things are a matter of professional judgment," the doctor continued, trying to extricate himself from the web of accusation he had spun. "There is a wide range of symptoms in these cases that can be interpreted in different ways."

He was backtracking, trying to diffuse his prior criticism.

"Observation during the night may not have led to such a severe diagnosis. Your son's breathing may have declined over a few short hours and worsened rapidly. There's no exact science in these situations, and the medical profession must rely on their subjective experience.

"I'm aware of a test, especially for C-section babies, that's under development. It's initially been shown to determine if the lungs of a fetus are mature and able to breathe on their own. Unfortunately, the test is in the early stages of research and not proven ready for use by practitioners.

"There is no culpability here, no blame. It's just one of those very unfortunate circumstances. I apologize for my prior remarks and hope that I didn't cause you any more distress."

"None of that matters, Doctor," I responded. "Can you tell me what happens now?"

"Sure, thank you for understanding. There really is nothing we can do medically to help your son beyond the treatment we've already provided. We're focusing on making him as comfortable as possible under the circumstances."

Just as Dr. Rice finished his sentence, the trembling in Matthew's hand stopped. His arm went limp. Looking up, I noticed that he was no longer struggling to breathe. His chest was at rest after having heaved so violently.

I caught the doctor's eyes. He slowly nodded as he closed them gently.

Matthew had died while I was at his side. At least he seemed more at peace, no longer shaking and gasping for breath. His pale pink color had taken on a bluish hue.

"Cyanosis. Not unusual for baby's suffering from HMD," was the explanation I received.

I stood by my son's side for a while, still holding his hand. It was slowly cooling, having lost the warmth of life. I was beyond crying. Bending over, I kissed him on the forehead of his now lifeless body.

Turning, I left the Infant Intensive Care Unit, my head down as I walked to the exit. When I reached the emergency entrance area, my brother and my mother were waiting for me. They had been informed by the medical staff of Matthew's passing. Mark grabbed me, hugging me with all of his might.

"I'm sorry." His eyes were moist. He was crazy about Sheila and me, and this new tragedy brought him to his knees. But he stayed strong for both of us.

"Come on. We followed in my car. I'll take you back to be with Sheila. Mom's coming too," he said.

"Thanks," I gurgled weakly.

My mother lightly touched my arm, trying to demonstrate

her support. She didn't utter a word. She had no idea how to express her grief.

I sat in the front passenger seat as my brother exited the parking lot, taking a major street on the way to Sheila's hospital. My mother was in the back seat. None of us spoke. There was nothing to say that could help. I was dreading the trip back, burning with the desire to see my wife without the delay of New York traffic. I was holding back my tears, but for whatever purpose, I still don't know today. I quietly sobbed at every stoplight. My mind was a blur. Everything and everyone seemed surreal.

After nearly an hour, we arrived at the hospital. The fact that it was not normal visiting hours precluded my mother and brother from proceeding beyond the waiting room. Those were the rather inflexible rules enforced by most hospitals in the late 1960s.

Sheila was a mess when I arrived in her room.

"I never even saw him," she said. "I never touched him. Never held him. Never kissed him. My arms feel so heavy; they ache from emptiness. I don't even know what my heart is feeling. I'm numb."

She began to cry, gently at first and then more heavily.

"I did get the chance to hold his hand. But I also watched him die. I kissed Matthew for both of us."

Then, even though I wanted to remain strong for Sheila, I joined her in weeping for our son. We held each other's hands as we let our emotions take charge.

Soon, she stopped.

"We can't do this. We need to be strong. We need to accept what life throws at us and be brave about it. No, not callous, not insensitive. Just strong, with our heads held high." Her eyes had grown bright, but they betrayed the deep feeling of pain underneath.

I looked at her with great admiration and squeezed her hand. Kneeling at her bedside, I kissed her face and lips. She felt cold.

My love for her had begun with initial attraction, but it was the strength and beauty of her character as well as her wonderful perspective on life that cemented it in place. And here she was displaying these again in the face of tragedy. She was the finest person I had ever known.

Then we heard the loud, abrasive words spoken by the woman sharing Sheila's room. "I already signed the papers putting her in foster care. Go away. Damn you, why do you keep bothering me? I won't take care of this baby. Never wanted to. Haven't fed her or held her yet. So just leave me alone and put her where you want."

"What the hell is that?" I whispered to Sheila.

"She never wanted her baby," Sheila answered. "She didn't even want to see her. She's given the baby away into the foster care system."

"What? And they put her in here in this room with you."

"I'm fine," Sheila said, waving my comment off with her right hand.

"Give me a minute," I said.

I stormed out of the room and approached the nurses' station.

"Do you people know what's going on with my wife? We lost our baby and you have her in a room with someone who doesn't care a lick for hers. She gave it away, in fact. And my wife has to hear all of this. What's the matter with you people? Don't you have any feelings for a person who just suffered our loss? Now, get her out of that room. My wife deserves better. Please, get her out of there now."

After lashing out, I struggled to hold on to any measure of self-constraint.

"Calm down, sir," said one of the nurses. "We don't have another room to move your wife to. We are so overloaded that some patients are in beds in the hallways on other floors. And that's not an option for your wife given her condition after surgery. There is really nothing we can do."

I bristled at the response.

A second nurse at the station added, "Anyway, that woman will be released in a day or two depending on her doctor's orders.

You'll see, things will be better then."

"Better then? I'm talking about now. And you people knew the situation with our first baby's death. How the hell did you put a woman who was giving her baby away in a room with my wife in the first place?"

"Perhaps that was an oversight. We're sorry. But we can't change anything now. So just quiet down, relax, and be patient. The situation will be fixed in a day or two."

"That's not acceptable to me. Who can I see that can take some action?"

"You might want to see one of the administrators who perhaps can override hospital practice and rules. But it is the weekend and they won't be in until Monday. And by then the woman will surely be gone."

"Humm," I said, seeing that I was getting nowhere.

It became apparent that there was nothing inherently sinister here, just judgment errors, some mistakes, and a lot of bureaucracy.

I quickly realized that my focus should be on returning to Sheila's bedside and continuing to address the tragedy at hand. Arguing about a room seemed trivial in that context. So I walked away from the nurses' station resigned to leave the room issue behind me and attend to my wife's needs.

That night, I made the many necessary phone calls to inform others close to us of our second baby's death. Those were tough calls. I could barely hold myself together for most of them. Usually, I hung up bawling, even though I tried with all my effort not to. Fortunately for me, my mother, brother, and a few close friends helped shoulder some of that load.

Over the next few days, Sheila was visited by our family and friends, who helped keep her spirits from sagging. My younger brother came to Sheila's room every day and night, most of the time ducking the limitation on guests beyond official visiting hours. Silently perched on the room's narrow windowsill, he would occasionally peer outside at the Brooklyn streets. Even though he rarely uttered a word, his presence was a great comfort to Sheila.

On a cold early spring day, our mother asked Mark why he spent so much time in the hospital just sitting at the window.

"'Cause I have to be there," was his complete explanation.

The time passed methodically by, which helped us begin to distance ourselves from our loss. Nevertheless, the healing process was painfully slow.

"I love you. We'll get through this. Our love will get us through this," Sheila assured me as we held each other day after day in the hospital.

Finally, the time came for Sheila's discharge. Fortunately, the woman in the next bed had left a number of days before.

As I was packing up Sheila's clothes and sundry items like perfume and a hairbrush, a short jovial gentleman with a reddish-blonde mustache entered the room. He was carrying a large box which he placed on Sheila's bed.

"Let's see what we've got here for you," he said. He began happily removing items from the box.

"Some baby formula, a few diapers for starters. And some baby powder."

"Hold it," I said. "Stop! Put those things back and please leave. We lost our baby."

"What? Oh, uh. I'm so sorry. I didn't know. We provide these things for all the new mothers leaving the hospital," he explained uncomfortably as he hurriedly repacked the box with the items he had placed on the bed.

"So sorry. So very sorry."

He left the room quickly without another word.

"It's okay," Sheila said with her head slightly bowed.

"We'd better get used to this. I guess some other people are going to make the same mistake."

I grabbed her as she stood by her bed and hugged her as tightly as I dared since her incision was still quite tender.

"Oh, I love you so much. I'm so glad you're in my life. You

make me so happy, even after all of this."

Sheila smiled at me as we walked slowly to the waiting wheelchair that would take her to the hospital exit.

*****

"You should sue the bastards," Sheila's uncle offered.

"That staff pediatrician didn't know what he was doing. Your baby should have received much more attention than he did. They should have noticed he was having breathing difficulties. The hospital was remiss in its duties. They let you two down and they should pay for it."

Sheila and I listened intently during her uncle's visit to our apartment. He was a very bright man with solid experience, and we respected his opinion.

"I know some lawyers who can get this suit going. I think it's worth a million or two at least. I'll bet that the hospital and the doctor will settle way before this thing goes to court. That will save both of you the pain of reliving your tragedy. You should really do this. The level of incompetence deserves it."

After an hour or so, he left our apartment still urging us to pursue a malpractice suit against the hospital and staff pediatrician. Given what I had heard from Dr. Rice, I was sure Sheila's uncle was on firm ground. It seemed that incompetence, lack of skill, and sloppiness were on display during Matthew's tribulations. Still, neither one of us wanted to become embroiled in a contentious situation. Mostly we viewed the potential gain as unseemly.

"Dirty money. That's how I see it. Dirty money," was Sheila's dismissal of a potential lawsuit.

"I would never feel comfortable with money earned from our son's death, even it was justified. It would always feel wrong."

We had given the issue much consideration and consistently arrived at the same conclusion.

"I agree," I declared.

That was the last time we talked about gaining economic benefit from our son's demise.

After coming home from the hospital, we were making some minor progress at putting the grim past behind us. Three weeks later, when I returned home from work, Sheila told me with watery eyes, "My grandma just passed away. You know that before Matthew died, she was in the old age home. Well, it seems that one of my uncles told her about Matthew. That night she tried to leave the building to come see us. The staff intercepted her, and because she wrestled with them to let her go, they were forced to put her in restraints. I'm guessing she just deteriorated from there."

"Damn," I exclaimed in frustrated sadness. "First my grandmother, and now yours."

*****

Standing at the table in our small kitchen, Sheila opened the official-looking envelope that had come in the day's mail. She read the contents slowly, lowering her head halfway through. Her sparkling eyes dimmed. A tear found its way down her cheek.

"What's the matter? What is it that? What does it say?"

Sheila didn't respond.

Sensing that my questions were making things worse, I hugged her around the waist, looking over her shoulder to see what had disturbed her.

"Damn it," I said. Peering at the document in Sheila's delicate hands, I immediately recognized Matthew's birth certificate.

"Don't those jackasses in the city hall of records have any brains? I guess they go through the motions without investigating anything. Do they have any idea how this document hurts?" I was angry and raising my voice.

"Nobody's fault," Sheila whispered. "They probably didn't receive notification of Matthew's death. It may have been an oversight by the hospital. Or maybe we screwed up and didn't file the correct papers."

"You're always willing to defend anyone, even it's someone who hurts you. That sweetness, kindness, is one of the reasons I love you so much."

Sheila smiled as my hug tightened around her middle.

Yet, I quickly returned to my original reaction. I didn't share my wife's tranquil forgiveness. Grabbing the paper from her hands, I was ready to crumble it up and throw it away.

"No, no. Don't ruin it." Sheila demanded.

"It's brought back bad memories, breaking my heart a second time. But at least it's something about our son that we can keep and cherish. Give it back to me, please. I'll put in a safe place."

"Of course," I said, gaining my composure through her words. I smiled and handed the document back to her,

"Damn, but you're wonderful," I proclaimed in a soft and admiring voice.

*****

"You've been spared the heartache of seeing your offspring in a withered state confined to an institution." Jimmy, my co-worker explained over lunch.

"Our child, Stacey, is deformed physically and impaired mentally. My wife and I feel like our lives have been turned on edge and spun around. We spend many nights and every weekend visiting the institution taking turns holding our hapless daughter. We can't really help beyond that because her care requires professional expertise. Nurses and attendants provide that. We feel hopeless in our ability to help, but we're still drawn to our daughter constantly.

"We talk about whether we're ignoring our other two children since we spend nearly all of our free time at the institution. Sometimes, we even find ourselves hoping for the final solution, Stacey's death. What a horrible thing. We hate ourselves for it. It's tearing us up inside, and we don't see any way out of our predicament. Every emotion, good and bad, passes through our hearts. We're confused, frustrated, sad, and don't know what to think anymore.

"I know how much it must hurt you and your wife to have lost two babies. But you may very well be better off in the long run not facing what we are. I know that this is tough to hear but try to keep your spirits up and look ahead. Ken, you and your wife may be able to put this tragedy behind you in the future. We can't. At least your situation may have a solution and a positive ending. That's an impossibility for my family."

I shared Jimmy's story with Sheila. She cried for him and for his wife.

"I'd like to help them. But I realize there's nothing we can actually do. Maybe it would help if we had dinner and listened to their story. Why don't you ask them, Ken?"

We both thought that in some odd way, we were fortunate.

The next few weeks were more peaceful for both of us, as peaceful as can be given the recent turn of events. We worked through our pain and sense of loss with the simple and objective acceptance of reality.

Sheila and I liked the apartment we were renting, furnishing, and decorating the three small rooms to meet our needs. Yet, we were never able to transform it into anything but a space from which children were absent. Our broken hearts searched for a way to satisfy our aching arms, filling the void with a baby to hold and cuddle.

We focused on the time ahead and our prospects for having a family. How would we navigate the shoals of uncertainty, our future hanging in the balance? We often wondered whether the bleak past was a portent of things to come, having children an elusive dream, never to become reality.

CHAPTER 4 -- A CHANGE IN DIRECTION

"Unfortunately, I must deny your request for this agency's services in adopting a child. Let me explain why; there are a number of reasons.

"First, we require proof that you're unable to have your own biological children. From what you have told me about your history, you will not be able to do so.

"Second, we have a waiting policy relating to parents who've experienced a tragedy, which you clearly have. This agency believes that it is too soon after the unfortunate events you recently went through. We require many more months, perhaps even years, for potential parents to heal and recover emotionally. Only the passage of time ensures that.

"And third, you can only adopt a child if they are of the same religion and race. This is done for the sake of the child. You did not indicate either on your initial application, implying to us that these issues are of no concern to you. And since you aren't specific about your religious preferences, we cannot meet your needs.

"I'm sure that if you have contacted other agencies, they've told you the same. I suspect you'd be told they couldn't help you because of your indifference toward religious commitment, as well as lacking the proof that you cannot have your own child.

"Also, like us, they undoubtedly would want much more time to pass from the date of your loss. Additionally, we know from our own experience in the field that the wait for a child from many agencies can be years."

This was the explanation we received from a neatly dressed, middle-aged woman with a well-heeled appearance. She was quite explicit about the conditions under which her adoption agency operated.

"We've contacted a number of adoption agencies of all sorts, and you're correct about the conditions being very similar, if not exactly the same as yours," Sheila commented with disappointment and frustration in her voice.

"But why does religion or race matter?" I questioned, tugging at my tie, which felt like it was choking me. "We don't care at all. It's of no concern to us, and it won't change a thing. Our love will be unconditional for any child in our care. And we'll raise that child to be healthy, safe, and most of all, happy, and of course, a solid, contributing citizen. The waiting period you described makes no sense; we're ready now, and I believe only we can determine that, not someone else. As far as not being able to have our own biological child, I don't see how that should affect a person's ability to adopt and care for an unwanted child. Why place these arbitrary restrictions on the process?"

I was perplexed by the agency adoption process and reacted to being stymied by what I thought was establishment nonsense. I felt blocked at our futile attempts to adopt. I knew Sheila shared my sense of being thwarted at every turn.

"If I may, I will object to the word arbitrary. Our policies have been in place for years. They are tried and true and have been tested many times. They work quite well and are in place for the benefit and protection of our babies."

Sheila and I had heard similar words from all of the adoption agencies we had visited over the past few months. It was a common theme, so we realized there was no purpose in continuing our meeting.

"Thank you," Sheila said to the woman behind the large oak desk. She slowly stood up out of her chair.

"Come on, Ken, let's go."

"All right," I replied. I stood and took her hand.

When we were outside, Sheila spoke with conviction, echoing my sentiments.

"Why does religion or race matter to everyone else, except us? We haven't specified or even raised it. Not once. Neither of us cares. Isn't a child a child, no matter what the situation? And why is it too soon, and why do we need to prove we're infertile? Who comes up with these limiting conditions?"

"I'm just miserable about the whole thing," Sheila summed it up.

We left the adoption agency with the same frustration we had experienced in all the others we had contacted. It was now a great disappointment after we had decided that the best course of action for us was to adopt a child.

A number of months had passed since Matthew's death, and our flagging spirits were getting the best of us. Aching for a baby to hold and cherish, we thought that adoption would meet our driving desire. We recognized we were not mainly motivated by altruism, but we also believed that our loving home would be a fine place to raise a child otherwise abandoned.

"I think we can give so much. So very much. And we might actually be whole again," Sheila said.

After leaving the agency, the last on our list, we drove home with a feeling of emptiness and defeat. It seemed that we failed at every attempt to bring a child into our lives. Whatever hope we had shriveled into disappointment and despair, frustration curdling in our veins. We felt like strangers in a foreign land.

"What do we do now? Is there nowhere to turn?" Sheila

asked. There would be no answer to her questions. "What do we have to do? Who can we speak to? What do you think, Ken? Can you think of someone who can guide us?"

"Let's talk with Phil. He may very well have an answer for us." Phil was my older brother and a Rabbi.

*****

"Sure, I think that I can help you," Phil explained on the phone.

"There's a process in New York, governed by state law, that allows for what is termed a private adoption. I've seen your frustration trying to go through agencies, and I've been waiting for you to ask me. I'm so glad you did. I just didn't want to interfere with what you were doing. You know, sticking my two cents in where it may not belong. But I'm really glad you called."

"Well, stick your two cents in now. We need it." I responded with an attempt at some humor.

"These legal private adoptions are handled by lawyers who specialize in the area. I'll check around and call you in a few days when I get some information."

"Thanks so much, Phil. You've given us hope. We should have contacted you sooner."

"Forget it. You did what you had to do, and now we'll go from here. You know that I hurt terribly for you and Sheila over the past few months, and now I'm glad to help in some way. But please don't get too excited until I make some calls."

"Thanks again, Phil. We look forward to hearing from you."

I hung up the phone and explained the possible solution to Sheila.

"Your brother is a great guy," she declared.

Sheila grabbed me around for a giant hug. Her eyes were watery as we kissed lovingly.

"Maybe someone will fulfill our dreams."

The phone rang a few days later.

Sheila answered it. "Hi, Phil."

I leaned close to the receiver to listen.

Phil said, "Well, I've got some information for you. I think you'll find it good news. Have you got some paper and a pen handy?"

"Hang on just a second," Sheila said and grabbed a pen and paper from a drawer in our kitchen. "Okay. Go ahead."

"I have the name of a private adoption lawyer who may be perfect for you guys. His name is Seymour Fenton. Let me spell that for you.

"I've given him your names and phone number. I've also explained your situation to him. He was very sympathetic and is pretty sure he can help. He'll call you in a few days. I've got to run. Good luck and let me know how things turn out."

"Thanks so much," Sheila said as she hung up the phone.

We hugged tightly. This was the first positive news we had in a few months. Cautious smiles widened our faces.

*****

"Here we are," I pointed out after checking the house number against the piece of paper Sheila held in her hand. The directions Seymour Fenton had provided over the phone when he had called were perfect.

"How do I look?" Sheila asked. She had left our car and was standing near it on the street. Her hands moved downward along her torso, straightening her dress.

"You look great, as usual. Hey, this isn't a fashion contest."

"Yeah, but look at you all dressed up in a suit and tie. You look even better than when you go to work. I guess we're really trying to impress this guy any way we can."

"As nervous as we are, let's just be ourselves."

"Wouldn't know any other way to be. So let's do this."

We walked directly to the front door of a modest house and rang the bell.

"Hello. I'm Seymour Fenton, but please just call me Seymour."

We were greeted by a short, stocky man who had opened the door. His ruddy complexion was quite noticeable, as was his well-dressed appearance.

"Come on in," he said as he closed the door behind us. "Let's have a seat in the living room where we can be comfortable and conduct our business. Would you like something to drink?"

"No thank you," Sheila and I answered simultaneously.

"Well then, we can proceed directly with the business at hand, Ken and Sheila. Oh, may I call you by your first names?"

"Sure," I confirmed.

"So Ken, your brother has informed me that you're interested in a private adoption. I certainly can help you with that. I'm an attorney, and I have legal connections all over the country who represent women who want to give their baby away. Once they contact me, the process is simple. You just go pick up the child."

"That's it?" Sheila was surprised at how uncomplicated it sounded.

"Well, of course, there are the appropriate papers to be completed and filed with the state court and social services. But I'll handle that. You don't even need to be involved except to sign your names.

"There's also the matter of the probationary period. The child will live in your house or apartment for six months before you can appear before a New York State judge to finalize the adoption. During that period of time, the birth mother has the option to change her mind. And you'll be screened by Social Services, including at least one visit to your residence. This is to ensure you're caring for the baby properly and that you're fit parents."

"Wow, both of those things sound really serious. Looks like they can be troublesome hurdles to jump over and can lead to potential problems," Sheila said.

"Yeah, I agree." I was beginning to feel a sense of uncertainty about the whole process.

"Don't worry," Seymour responded. "I've been through this

many times and both issues rarely present a problem, if ever. Leave everything to me. I handle any problem that comes up. All you have to worry about is being great parents. Meeting with both of you and knowing your backgrounds, that won't be an issue at all. You'll sail through with social services. Everything always goes smoothly without a hitch, and it will for the two of you. Don't worry about a thing. Of course, all of this is contingent on you following every one of my instructions to the letter in all the details."

It was obvious that Seymour suffered no fools.

Seymour's assurances were somewhat helpful. But they were almost too good, too absolute. Some of his words sounded like a salesman with the "No doubt about it" and "It's in the bag" routine. But we were at the end of our rope for answers. We had to trust him and believe what he said.

"Of course, then there's the issue of price," Seymour continued.

"Price?" Sheila asked. "How does that work?"

"Well, it's customary for the adopting parents to reimburse the birth mother for her hospital fees and other associated expenses. Additionally, payment for her efforts on your behalf is also expected. I will negotiate that with her attorney. Of course, I will expect compensation for services rendered and the other attorney's fees. That's it."

"How much does the total cost amount to?" I asked rather sheepishly. I didn't want to come across as concerned about money rather than the adoption itself.

"That depends on a number of things. But you shouldn't concern yourself with those now. Suffice it to say somewhere between three thousand and five thousand dollars covers all the costs of the transaction."

Sheila and I looked at each other.

Seymour made it all sound so cold and bureaucratic. The future of a human life was in the balance, and many different emotions were involved on each side. We realized, though, that this was his trade, his profession. He had managed the process many times before. Oddly, we both felt comfortable with his stolid, businesslike approach.

"All right then," Seymour concluded. "It was a pleasure meeting both of you. As soon as you decide to move forward, just let me know and I can begin the process. Based on past experience, it should move pretty quickly."

"Thanks," flowed from our lips in unison.

Both of us had major concerns as we left Seymour's house. During the short walk to our car, we didn't speak, trying to process what had transpired.

The silence was broken once I pulled away from the curb into traffic.

"A six-month waiting period when the mother can change her mind." I could barely hear Sheila's unsettled voice. "That's something I sure don't want to go through."

"The sword of Damocles hanging over our heads," I agreed.

"After all we've been through, can we handle that level of uncertainty? It's going to be a tough six months."

"Seymour was pretty confident, though. And he sure seems like he knows what he's doing," Sheila seemed to think out loud, starting to address her issues.

"We'll just have to trust in him," I responded.

"It'll be difficult, but we'll get through it. I know we can." Sheila's stalwart personality was shining through.

"But," I began, "the cost is out of our league, and despite the fact that we're both well-paid professionals by any standard. We don't have any savings yet since we just started out. Where are we going to get that kind of money?"

"Maybe a loan. But I don't think banks are going to let us borrow that much cash without collateral, and we don't have any. I'm pretty sure we can pay the money back over time based on our earnings, but from what I know about banks, it won't be easy to secure a loan."

"Well, we'll just have to try."

We became quiet again. Thoughts of how we would handle the issues flooded my consciousness and, no doubt, Sheila's, too. When we returned to our apartment, we talked deep into the night, exploring possibilities and sharing our feelings.

*****

The phone rang. I picked it up.

"Hi, it's Phil. I got your call earlier but couldn't talk. Tell me, how did you make out with Seymour Fenton?"

"It went well."

I proceeded to tell my older brother we were thrilled with the prospects of adopting a baby. After sharing our concerns about the six-month waiting period and the social services review first, I mentioned the money issue. Three to five thousand dollars was a great deal of money in 1970, especially for young people just starting out.

"I agree. It's a lot of money. But I think I can help. Linda's parents have given us a wedding gift which is more than we need. I'd be happy to give you a loan. No interest, no strings attached. You pay me back when you can."

"Wow." I was so excited at my brother's offer. I knew his wife's parents had money, but I didn't realize he had benefited from it.

"Thanks, Phil. Thanks so much. Are you positive? Are you sure that you don't need that money? Really sure?"

"Yep," was the terse reply. "It's yours if you need it. It's Linda's and my pleasure to help you two out."

I hung up the phone after thanking Phil again.

"You're not going to believe this." I was nearly yelling at Sheila with joy. "Phil has some money from his in-laws and has offered to give us a loan for the cost of the adoption. Is that great, or what?"

Sheila jumped into my arms and kissed me. I had never felt her grip so strong.

"What terrific news," she whispered into my ear, nearly sobbing with happiness. "Please give me the phone. I want to call your brother and tell him how much we appreciate his offer. This is going to make things so much easier."

*****

"Hello, Sheila. This is Seymour Fenton," the voice said on the other side of the phone as I listened in again. It was Thursday, July 2, 1970. "A girl was born this morning in a small town in Upstate New York. I've been contacted by the birth mother's attorney, and if you agree, you can drive up this coming Monday and pick up the baby."

Sheila was so excited, she fell silent while processing the information.

"Hello, are you there?" Seymour inquired.

"Yes, Seymour. Of course we agree. Thank you," she responded after a few moments.

"Good. Now listen carefully. You must have a mature person with you who the baby will be handed to. You are not to see or meet the birth mother, so as to be in compliance with New York State law, which dictates that neither party should be aware of the other's identity. And things always work better that way. Keeps emotions to a minimum and helps to keep the mother on track, avoiding undo ambivalence, now and over the next few months. Although, again, let me emphasize to you that she is totally free to change her mind at any time over the next six months. That is important for you to understand and accept."

"Yes, we understand that aspect quite well."

"Okay, then. You should consider purchasing a baby outfit for the child in case the hospital doesn't supply one. It probably will be quite warm on a summer's day so choose accordingly. Also, have a bottle or two of baby formula with you for the long ride home and some extra wipes and diapers."

"Write down this address. I'll meet you there at noon on Monday. And lastly, get a bank check for thirty-five hundred dollars to be handed to me when you arrive. Now here are the directions."

"See you at noon on Monday," Sheila concluded after writing down the information and thanking Seymour again.

She jumped into my arms and then repeated the instructions she had just received.

We discussed the particulars at length that night. First, we decided that the person who should accompany us would be Sheila's friend, Marilyn.

"It would be my pleasure," Marilyn told us as she gladly agreed to serve in the role of the baby receiver.

"I'll even wear my dental hygienist whites," Marilyn proposed. This would make her look like a professional nurse.

"We'll borrow Dad's car. Not use ours. The Dodge is four years old, a smaller mid-size, and we've had those engine problems. My parent's car is a newer, full-size sedan, and it's the first automobile they've ever owned. It's immaculate. The newer larger car will make the trip more comfortable and reliable," I explained to Sheila. "My brother Mark offered to drive, leaving me free to enjoy the baby with you in the back seat on the long trip home."

"Sounds like a solid plan. I'm so very excited just talking about it."

On Saturday morning, we visited the bank to which Phil had wired the required money. Afterward, we bought the baby supplies Seymour had outlined. We tried to remain cool all weekend, but the sense of anticipation kept us wound-up for Monday.

*****

"Hi. Get in and let's get going," Mark said through a rolled-down window as he leaned across the front seat. He had pulled up to the curb in front of our apartment building. It was five in the morning on Monday.

Marilyn, who had driven to our apartment earlier, Sheila, and I opened the doors of my parent's shining sedan and got in. Marilyn sat in the front seat with Mark while Sheila and I loaded our baby supplies into the back and sat down. The black Plymouth sparkled in the early morning sun as Mark pulled out, heading toward Manhattan and then to the New York State Thruway.

"Too early for heavy rush hour traffic," Mark said.

"Just as we planned. We should have no problem making the noon meeting Upstate. It's almost a five-hour drive and we've given ourselves over six hours. We should be there early," he concluded.

The trip went smoothly. Some light conversation, mostly between Marilyn and Sheila, helped pass the time. Otherwise, we were quiet, all trying to contain our sense of excitement.

"Here we are," Mark declared as he pulled into an older strip shopping center. "The attorney's office is in here somewhere."

"There it is," Marilyn said, pointing to a storefront with a sign listing four last names with an "and" before the last. Mark steered the car to a parking space right in front of the office. He quickly checked the time.

"Yep, just as I said, a full hour early."

We exited the large sedan and headed to the attorney's office.

"Wow, you're early," said the receptionist. "Have a seat. May I offer you some coffee?"

"Sure," we all said, looking forward to some refreshment after the long early morning trip.

The receptionist returned with four cups of coffee on a tray.

"Cream and sugar are on the table behind you." She pointed as she handed each of us a cup. "Mr. Fenton isn't here yet, and neither is our partner in charge. Please just relax. I'm sure they both will be here soon."

After fifteen minutes, Seymour arrived. He was a bit frenetic as he greeted us curtly.

"In here, Mr. Fenton," the receptionist directed. Seymour disappeared behind an office door. The office was occupied by a very well-dressed middle-aged man who had entered a few minutes before, and whom the receptionist had greeted in an obsequious tone.

A half-hour passed, and Seymour came out of the office.

"Good to see you all. And you are?"

"Marilyn," Sheila answered for her friend. "Sorry we didn't introduce you before, but you seemed in such a hurry."

"Fine. No problem."

"I'm going to take Marilyn to the hospital where the baby is. The three of you wait about ten minutes and then drive to the parking lot at the hospital's main entrance. I gave you the directions. Right?"

"Right." Mark and I responded.

"Okay then. Marilyn, my car is just outside. Let's go."

They both disappeared quickly into Seymour's upscale automobile and sped away.

We waited the stated ten minutes and headed outside to our car, thanking the receptionist for her hospitality as we left.

"Crap. Damn. Can't get it to start," Mark cursed loudly as he tried the starter over and over. He turned the key in the ignition again and again, but nothing happened except a loud cranking noise emanating from the engine.

"I'll get out and look under the hood," he said, slamming the driver's side door behind him.

"You guys try and stay calm. Don't come out to help. You don't want to get full of grease and dirt."

Mark raised the hood and looked at the engine with great agitation on his face.

"This car is practically new. Just out of the showroom. Hasn't had a problem before. Now of all times, it acts up," he mumbled as if he was talking to the motor.

Touching various parts of the engine, pulling on wires, and checking fluid and oil levels, Mark performed his own brand of automotive inspection.

"I think I got it," he yelled at us in the car with a smile on his face. "The carburetor baffle was stuck."

Rushing, he closed the engine hood with a smash, swung around the front bumper, ripped the driver's door open, and jumped into the front seat.

"There she goes." He grinned happily as he turned the ignition key victoriously. A loud whooshing sound filled the cab when the engine turned over. We all smiled, the engine humming with power.

"How long did that take?" Mark asked, looking at his watch.

Reality set in. Our momentary gratification was quickly replaced by a gripping angst. Seymour and Marilyn had left for the hospital over a half-hour before, and we hadn't even left the attorney's parking lot.

"Let's go, Mark. Throw her in gear and head to the hospital pronto," I told him, an unnecessary command since the car was already in motion. Mark had backed out of our parking spot and was speeding toward the parking lot exit.

"Don't get us all killed," Sheila said half-seriously as she tried to lighten the mood.

Fifteen minutes later, we entered the hospital grounds. Mark wheeled the car into a parking space at the front entrance of the hospital, just as Seymour had directed.

We looked around, not knowing what to expect. What would happen next? Were we too late?

We waited. To prevent any other mechanical mishaps, Mark left the car running. He avoided putting on the air conditioning so as not to tax the engine.

Fifteen minutes passed slowly. The searing heat of a hot summer day in the sun boiled the cab, making our wait more uncomfortable than it already was.

"Look, it's Marilyn," Sheila pointed excitedly to the exit door of the hospital.

"She sure looks like she's carrying a baby in that blanket. Seymour is right behind her."

Marilyn walked carefully toward the car, her head down, looking at the bundle she was holding. As she approached our car, she raised her head looking directly at us. A wide grin broke out across her lips.

"Get in," said Seymour. He had opened our car door.

Marilyn bent down carefully and handed her parcel to Sheila in the back seat. She then hurriedly opened the passenger side door and sat down. Turning her head, Marilyn glanced back at her friend. Her warm eyes gleamed with great satisfaction. "You look like you were meant for this."

I looked at Sheila holding our new baby. I felt so tranquil and sanguine.

Seymour knocked on the window. "Congratulations. Now it's time for you to go. The birth mother will be coming out soon," he said, pointing frenetically toward the exit with his gnarled hand.

Mark turned the car around and headed back to the New York Thruway for the long trip home.

I looked back. Seymour was gone.

"She's more beautiful than I ever expected," Sheila said as she peeled back the blanket in which the infant was wrapped. We had already decided to name her Kim.

"And the mother has her dressed in a lovely layette. What a nice gesture."

The ride home was a joyous one. Sheila beamed through the whole trip. Kim cried a few times and Sheila supplied the usual pacifier treatment or fed her some formula from the bottles we had prepared before the trip. Everything seemed so serene.

When the car arrived in front of our apartment building, we thanked Marilyn and Mark one last time. Taking the elevator, we entered our small three rooms. Sheila placed Kim in the crib we had set up in our living room, and she immediately fell asleep. Exhausted, we headed to our bedroom just to lie down.

"I love you so much. I'm so very happy right now," Sheila said. We snuggled together, holding on tight. Our lips met in a sweet embrace.

"I'm going to sleep on the couch tonight. I want to be close to Kim and not a room away. Also, it'll be easier to get the formula from the refrigerator in the kitchen. She'll probably need to be fed every four hours when she wakes up. And this way you can have a decent night's sleep since you have to go to work tomorrow. I want you to be rested."

Her concern for my welfare was emblematic of Sheila's kind and caring nature. Always concerned about other people's needs, especially mine, she frequently placed those needs before her own.

"If that's what you want. I do need the sleep to be ready for the office. Thanks. But please wake me if you need help."

Sheila just smiled with contentment. Her brilliant eyes were coming back to life from the pain they had experienced these past two years. Her face was tranquil.

After a week or so, Sheila was feeling the effects of little sleep and the daily routine of baby care. We worked together in organizing her activities more efficiently, which helped. She began to slowly gain her energy back, especially when Kim started to sleep through part of the night.

The next few months passed without incident. Kim was growing rapidly, and we felt like we had joined all of our close friends—as parents. Diaper boxes and baby paraphernalia filled the living room. The smell of baby powder permeated our apartment.

*****

"She's going to love this one," Sheila proclaimed as I showed her the yellow rubber bird that made a tweeting sound when squeezed. I had brought it home after work. Every week, I visited a toy store near my office in Manhattan, purchasing a new toy for Kim. I gleefully carried them with my attaché case onto the subway platform.

Crowded among the many people waiting for the express train to Brooklyn, I would gaze around chuckling to myself, "Hey look at me. I'm a father, like most normal folks, and I just bought a new toy for my daughter. It's here in this bag."

We had felt so different from other young couples at times. Situations like this helped us reattach to others of our generation.

Soon, our apartment was filled with toys, blocks, mobiles, and stuffed animals of all kinds.

I also enjoyed buying small gifts for Sheila. My special favorites were pieces of art depicting the love between a mother and child.

"This is just beautiful. What a wonderful gift, Ken," Sheila said, holding the blue glass statue of a child in the warm embrace of its mother. "This is going to have a special place of honor." Sheila placed it gently on her dresser in our bedroom. "Now I'll see it when I go to sleep at night and first thing when I wake in the morning." Then she turned and gave me a big Sheila hug.

*****

"I don't know if this picture tops the glass sculpture or not. I'm crazy about both of them," my wife said, expressing her appreciation for her newest gift. I had seen a marvelous print of a mother with her arms wrapped lovingly around her baby. Her face glowed. The frame perfectly highlighted the feeling the picture evoked.

"Please, Ken, hang it right here on the living room wall." Sheila pointed to just the right spot for the picture. "If you keep this up, the apartment will be overflowing with mother and child artwork. I'm thrilled. You know I adore you." With that, she pecked me on the cheek.

"I hope our good luck never takes a holiday," I wished, smiling at my own words.

In the evening after work and on weekends, at every opportunity, I delighted in playing with Kim. Touching her tiny hands and fingers, tickling her to make her laugh, or hiding a toy and making it reappear for her were some of our favorites.

I relished the times when I would hold her raised over my head, her body and legs stretched out parallel to the floor like she was flying. I tossed her gently in the air, releasing her for a moment, perhaps six inches at the most, and caught her on the way down with my arms extended upward. She would giggle and giggle.

Sometimes as I looked up, her saliva dribbled into my mouth. To me it was ambrosia.

CHAPTER 5 -- WAITING

"We're halfway through the six months," I announced one morning.

Although we were happily passing the days as new mother and father, the time was still clouded by the six-month probationary period during which the birth mother could change her mind. The potentially problematic issue of a social services review added to the unsettled nature of our situation. Our happiness was somewhat dampened by these concerns.

We had been waiting for the appointment for a week or so, knowing social services reviews were normally scheduled somewhere in the fourth month of the six-month waiting period.

After she hung up the phone, Sheila told me the social worker would arrive around eleven in the morning on Wednesday, and I had to make sure I was home.

Sheila said, "The review should take no more than an hour."

"Put that there. Clean under the couch. Throw that away. Vacuum that part of the carpet again." Sheila was directing us the morning of the meeting with social services.

"We need to make sure everything is spic and span. Spotless. You know we have to show like a model mom and dad. Whatever that is. Now Ken, put on your best suit and I think we'll be ready."

The anticipation of the meeting was building as the appointment time arrived. We had been on edge for a number of days. It felt like we were two pieces of meat on display in a butcher shop that would be examined by potential buyers. We would be scrutinized for whatever criteria applied for adoptive parents.

"Let's just be ourselves and take this in our stride. We're two good people who have been taking care of our baby quite well. So what could the social worker possibly see that's negative?"

"I'm with you," I agreed.

Within an hour the doorbell rang. I went to open it.

"Hello. My name is Betty Wolf. I'm a social worker with the Department of Social Services. I believe you're expecting me."

"Hello. Come right in and please have a seat." I motioned with my hand to the kitchen table next to where Sheila was standing. Clearly visible, there was a setting of three coffee cups and saucers, our best ones, accompanied by a home-baked chocolate cake and some cookies on a tray. Spoons and forks were neatly placed appropriately as was a creamer and a sugar bowl. They all sat on a lovely white tablecloth. Sheila had seen to every detail.

"Thank you," Betty said, sitting down at a place setting.

Betty was a bit dowdy but seemed like a good-natured soul as she smiled kindly at the two us.

"Chocolate cake, my favorite. This is entirely unnecessary, but it's been a while since I've had breakfast, so I appreciate it."

"Cream and sugar, Mrs. Wolf?" Sheila asked after cutting a slice of cake and placing it softly on the social worker's plate.

"Yes, thank you. And please, call me Betty. We need not be so formal. May I also refer to you by your first names?"

"Of course."

The meeting was beginning in an informal fashion, removing some of the tension turning our stomachs. Still, we had no idea what was to come or what was expected of us.

"Let me go over your backgrounds a bit," Betty began. "I've already reviewed your financial status based on the information that the department provided. It looks fine.

"Now just to review, Sheila, you are a registered dental hygienist licensed by the State of New York. And Ken, you work for a major pharmaceutical company in Manhattan as a Research Analyst in the Personnel and Industrial Relations Department. Is that correct?"

"Yes. That's right."

We both were aware that this information had been provided in advance. Betty was well aware of our professional positions. As we would discuss later, it seemed to both of us as if she was engaging in small talk to pass the time. That was fine with us.

"Ken, do you have a picture of your daughter in your wallet? And may I see it."

I pulled my wallet from the side pocket of my suit jacket, opened it, and showed Betty the two pictures of Kim in the clear plastic slide section.

"Nice photos." Betty reacted. "Thank you. Okay then. Would you mind showing me around your apartment?" Betty addressed Sheila.

"Well, it's small but cozy I like to say," Sheila started as she rose from the table.

"Small matters little. Cozy is nice." Betty slid her chair back under the table after standing and proceeded to follow Sheila into our bedroom.

"You've seen the kitchen. This is our bedroom."

Betty took only two steps into the room, looked around, and said, "Very nice bedspread. I like the colors. Very pretty. Matches the drapes well."

She turned, passed Sheila, and stopped back in the kitchen.

"Would you like to see our baby, Kim, now?" Sheila asked. We thought that might have been the first order of business before the apartment tour.

"Since I know this is a one-bedroom, three-room apartment, your daughter must be in the living room. Right?"

"That's right. You'll see that it's a long room. We've divided it so that our couch and two chairs are at one end, and Kim's crib and everything else she needs fit easily into the other," Sheila explained almost apologetically.

"That's fine," Betty said.

She walked by our furniture at the beginning of the living room and stopped at the crib at the end of the room. Kim was sound asleep. Betty bent her head, looked at her quickly, and then headed back to the kitchen.

"Well that's all I need," said Betty. "May I use your bathroom before I leave? I believe we passed it outside your bedroom."

"Certainly," Sheila pointed to the closed door of our bathroom.

We were both relatively sure that using the bathroom was an excuse to inspect it for cleanliness and hygiene.

"Goodbye," Betty said. "I think everything here is in good order. It was nice meeting you both."

After she left, Sheila and I breathed a sigh of relief. The review had not been as rigorous as we somehow expected. In fact, it had seemed rather perfunctory. Betty appeared to be a kind, gentle person whose closing remarks filled us with hope. We hugged each other warmly.

*****

"Hi, Mister Fenton." Sheila exchanged salutations with Seymour who was on the phone. I could imagine his gravelly voice.

"We're only a few weeks away from the court date with our daughter. We've been following all the press and television coverage of the Baby Lenore case. Given what's going on, I thought I would check in with you to make sure that everything is on track."

I leaned my head in close to Sheila's to listen. "It sure is. You know, I've been waiting for your call. I fully expected that with all the publicity around this case you would have some concerns. I was thinking of calling you first but thought the better of perhaps raising unnecessary worry.

"Be aware that there are many complications in the Baby Lenore case that make it quite different from your situation. In fact, it's so different, comparisons can't be made. Of course, as I mentioned to you before, the birth mother changing her mind is highly unusual. It has never happened in my experience and knowledge base.

"Rest assured that we have no glitches, and we are proceeding forward smoothly. Don't fret and don't be nervous. We're okay."

"Thanks. It helps to hear that right now."

"I'll see you at the Brooklyn Courthouse three weeks from now. I'll call you when I find out the exact time. I should know within the next few days."

Sheila felt a bit more relaxed after talking with Seymour. We had expected to be on edge during the six-month probationary period. The Baby Lenore case had raised our concerns since it focused on a birth mother's change of heart.

"It doesn't appear that we should have any concerns." Sheila reminded me. "Seymour is very confident."

"That's great news. Maybe we don't have anything to worry about." But I really wasn't so sure.

My desire was to help Sheila maintain her optimism fed by the conversation with Seymour. Still, I didn't want her to view the world only through rose-colored glasses, so that if some remote possibility developed, she would be totally and devastatingly crushed. She was the eternal optimist and I was a confirmed skeptic. We had always shared our thoughts about situations, outlining our opposite approaches, helping both of us to achieve a more balanced perspective.

Although I was hesitant to risk the chance of dashing Sheila's hopes, I felt the need to continue with the way we had in the past, an essential pillar of our relationship. And this time should be no exception. Anyway, my wife was as solid a human being as there was and had consistently shown that she could handle difficult situations with grace and composure. So I decided to share my thoughts with Sheila.

"I realize that Seymour thinks we're in the clear." I began. "It's an inherent part of his job to be positive and address his clients' issues. You know I'm skeptical about predictions of events until they actually happen. Yogi Berra said 'It ain't over till it's over,' and I agree. How can Seymour be so absolutely certain with three weeks still remaining in the waiting period? Of course, that's not at all to say something will happen with our adoption."

"Go ahead, Ken," Sheila said. "I can tell you have a lot more to say. I always welcome your thoughts and views. I still need to hear them."

As usual, my wife displayed her openness for information and her steadiness in handling anything.

So with Sheila's encouragement, I dismissed any reservations I had and continued on. I decided to review the case with her to make sure we were on the same page in our understanding.

"I know that the Baby Lenore case is complex and involves an adoption agency. In fact, it's the agency's actions that created much of the controversy in the case. They initially resisted the birth mother from reclaiming her baby in a relatively short time after she had given up her child for adoption. That created the adversarial relationship that fueled the case.

"I'm pretty sure they denied the birth mother even though her request was within the six-month probationary period. To make matters worse, they didn't inform the adopting parents of the birth mother's request until into the fifth month of the six months. By then those parents were deeply attached to the baby as their own.

"As I understand it, the mother filed suit in New York County Supreme Court against the agency. The adoptive parents were denied legal representation during the court's deliberations. As a result of all this, they fled to Florida with the baby, receiving a more favorable ruling from the court there.

"What an incredible mess," I summed up. "Who knows who's right or wrong. Regardless of the fact that all these complications don't apply to us, I still don't see how Seymour can be so positively certain."

I knew my wife wouldn't share all of my skepticism.

"Thanks," Sheila said. "That was very helpful. Of course, you know it has raised my anxiety. But I can handle it. Reality and caution are more important."

*****

"Here's a lollipop, little one. My, she is cute," said the judge.

Kim swiped the candy from his hand. The cellophane wrapper had been removed, so Kim put the sugary treat in her mouth and smiled.

We were in a large courtroom. The judge, dressed in the standard long black robe, sat behind a podium on a raised platform. We stood in front of the podium looking up at the judge's face and shoulders, the only visible part of his anatomy.

"You can put her down in the baby seat." The judge instructed Sheila who had been holding Kim in her arms.

"Now that the six-month required probationary waiting period has expired, you are here to officially and definitively have Kim Frances declared your daughter. Those are the first and middle names you've chosen for your daughter, correct?"

"Yes," we both answered simultaneously.

We had named her Kim Frances after our grandmothers, both of whom seemed to have been taken by our babies' deaths.

"You have passed the scrutiny of the Department of Social Services which has deemed you to be adequate and stable parents. From what I have observed in this courtroom this morning, I agree with the department's assessment. Please raise your right hands. Sheila, Ken, do you understand the obligations and responsibilities that parents assume for their children?"

"Yes."

"And are you prepared and ready willingly to provide that care to Kim Frances who you are about to adopt in the State of New York?"

"Yes."

"Then under the rules of New York State law, in the eyes of New York's citizens, and under the power vested in this Court, I hereby order and declare that Kim Frances is your child in perpetuity."

We stood for a moment, not knowing if the proceedings were concluded.

"Congratulations! That's it," the judge informed us.

"Thank you so much, Judge."

I hugged a beaming Sheila so hard I nearly stopped her breathing.

"I love you, MOM," I said, emphasizing Sheila's new official status. Tears of joy were evident flowing down her cheeks. It brought me such pleasure to see her this way.

"Thanks, DAD," she responded in kind. I was grinning from ear to ear.

"You may take your child and leave the court," the judge suggested, growing slightly impatient with our display of happiness. Other couples were waiting their turn to become parents for the first time.

CHAPTER 6 – THE PARK BENCH

"What a beautiful baby," a passerby exclaimed as she peeked inside the pram Sheila was pushing along Kings Highway, one of the main streets in Brooklyn.

The woman looked up at Sheila and then lowered her head so she could see Kim's face again in the carriage.

"She must get those big hazel eyes and striking blonde hair from her dad. I'll bet she looks just like her father," the woman declared. Sheila just smiled.

My wife is a tiny lady with black hair and shining dark brown eyes. Her face is fairly narrow, and many people assume that she is of southern Italian heritage. Kim, in contrast, was big-framed with a wide face, button nose, full lips, and Nordic coloring.

Sheila told me later that after the woman walked away, she leaned over and whispered to Kim, "We may not look alike. But you and I are mother and daughter, joined in that relationship for as long as we live. My love for you is way beyond any consideration of physical appearance, although you sure are beautiful, as the lady said." She neatened the blanket covering our daughter in the carriage. She couldn't be happier.

The next two years passed without incident. Thrilled with how things turned out, Sheila and I were so very pleased with our lives. Kim was the gateway to a new life.

"Is this great, or what?" were the words that passed from my lips as I stood in the doorway of our new apartment.

"It sure is great," echoed Sheila.

We were fortunate that my company moved us as part of their corporate relocation to central New Jersey. We escaped the crowded city. The area with so many farms and large areas of open space was just what we wanted. My commute to work was twenty minutes, and the apartment had most everything we were looking for: a nice kitchen, big living area, and two large bedrooms. To top it off, we had a lovely porch, so we could relax outside and even barbecue. And the complex even had a big pool, which I just knew we'd enjoy in the summer.

"It's all just wonderful." Sheila was as impressed with our good fortune as I was.

We spent the next year or so enjoying our new location. It seemed light years away from the city. Our families from Brooklyn visited on many weekends during which we shared our new lifestyle, including barbecues and splashes in the community pool.

"Well, that's the last check." Sheila smiled with a feeling of accomplishment and closure. We had not gone out for dinner, taken a vacation, or even went to a movie for over a year. Agreeing that we would repay my brother, Phil, with a monthly check, Sheila and I felt satisfied in our commitment to him and ourselves. We were diligent in sending him a check, like clockwork, at the beginning of every month.

"There's no need to pay me back in a certain amount of time," Phil had graciously told us when we had proposed the schedule we developed.

"You didn't have to let me know the schedule you're going to use. I don't need the money for anything, and I'm certainly not going to keep track of your payments. Paying me when you can is fine. No need to put yourself in a financial straitjacket."

We appreciated Phil's casual attitude about our loan. Nonetheless, Sheila and I were compelled by our value system. We needed to approach the economics of the situation with more attentiveness, ensuring our obligation and responsibility. That's just the way we did things.

Kim was growing like a weed. She was a very active child and began walking at ten months. A handful after that newly gained mobility, Sheila and I delighted in chasing her around the apartment, playing peek-a-boo and other games. We loved every minute spending time with our daughter, having fun with her at the pool, or picking fruit and vegetables at nearby farms. Her trove of toys continued to grow, now including puzzles, blocks, and children's books that we read to her every chance we had. It was a grand time.

Now that our lives were so full of joy and happiness, Sheila and I periodically reminisced about how it all began. Sometimes, before falling asleep, my mind would wander back to how we met.

"You look great. Go! Go! Hey. Hey."

"I love the way you dance in those sneaks."

"It's just a riot, Sheila."

Outside our apartment building in a sprawling complex, we had gathered around a park bench. My small group of friends had mingled with a larger group Sheila hung out with. Less than five feet tall, with tiny feet to match her small stature, she was having fun dancing the soft shoe in a friend's sneakers that were ten sizes too big. The large shoes flopped all over the walkway, making a smacking sound as her arms and feet swung back and forth.

"What a great beat," one of the gang exclaimed as we were all clapping loudly to accompany Sheila's movements. The words could barely be heard through the laughter and noise.

"Great fun, but I've got to stop now. I'm worn out," Sheila yelled in between her heavy breaths.

I was attracted to her immediately. Her black, flowing hair, beautiful chestnut brown eyes, and her radiant smile combined to complement her glowing happy face. She was giggling as she ended her dance, enjoying the moment to its fullest. As I would learn as we became lovers, this was Sheila's essence, embracing life to its fullest, always seeing the good in everything and enjoying all things and experiences, from the mundane to the profound.

"Well," she said, "I need to go upstairs now. I'm a little late for dinner. My mother is expecting me."

"Hey," I interjected, "I need to go upstairs for dinner too. I think we live in the same building. I'll go up with you. That is if you don't mind."

"Sure, I'd like that," she replied.

Was I ever excited. At eighteen years old, I didn't have much experience with introducing myself to girls. I had spent my high school days playing football, leaving me little time for socializing. Naturally shy and not outgoing, I lacked the skills needed in many situations. Now, when I had become a college freshman, a girl I was immediately attracted to seemed to accept my advances.

"Okay, this is my floor," Sheila announced as the elevator in our building reached the eighth floor.

"Bye," she said, her marvelous smile in full view.

"Bye," I responded awkwardly, not knowing how to carry the conversation further.

As she disappeared around the elevator bank, I smiled while watching her cute derriere wiggle in her tight shorts.

*****

"Great. What a really nice swing. You hit it straight and just the right distance."

Sheila and her friend had organized a pitch and putt golf outing with boys they were interested in. Sheila had selected me, and I couldn't have been more pleased. Although, being naïve, neither I nor the other guy suspected the girls' motivation.

"That was a lot of fun," Sheila's friend exclaimed after about two hours when we finished playing the short pitch and putt course.

"It sure was," the rest of us chimed in, laughing at our mutual ineptitude at the game.

"Let's go for something to eat."

We took a bus to a nearby burger joint. Conversing while we ate our burgers and fries accompanied by vanilla cokes, the four of us had more fun talking about the round we had just completed even more than actually having played. We joked and laughed for over two hours and then took another bus home.

"Goodnight," I said softly, gently kissing Sheila on the head in front of her apartment door. The smell of her hair was intoxicating. Without even realizing it, I was getting very attached to this girl, captivated, maybe even falling in love.

We spent the rest of the summer and the next few months seeing each other every day. We were both in college, attending separate divisions of the City University of New York in different locations.

"You take the F-Train, and I'll take the D-Train," Sheila and I would sing to the tune of a Scottish song. We spent our early mornings and then late afternoons commuting to school on the subway system snaking throughout Brooklyn.

"Let's hit Jerry's. I can taste the fresh hot doughnuts and chocolate milk."

"Sure, I'd like that. But can we stop at Nathan's first for a hot dog and a barbecue sandwich? I'm starving." I pleaded with Sheila, expanding her eating suggestions to include the famous eatery in Coney Island.

I was always hungry then. Petite Sheila, all 85 pounds of her, would indulge my hunger pangs with a chuckle of delight.

"Okay, we'll do Nathan's. And you can have one of those luscious cherry cheese knishes at Jerry's too."

"Great, let's eat," I proclaimed with joy.

Both Nathan's and Jerry's were located along the boardwalk area of Coney Island, an amusement area in the southern end of Brooklyn, situated along the Atlantic Ocean. The Coney Island beach was also quite famous in New York. Our vast towering apartment complex was located one block from these attractions, which were in differing states of decay and disrepair. In the sixties, Coney Island and our apartment complex were not considered desirable places to live.

"Let's sit and talk," Sheila suggested after many of our eating expeditions.

We both came from troubled homes. Our parents were challenged economically, and the strain of money issues, as well as a major mismatch in personalities and values, created trying homes to be raised in. Sheila's parents separated when she was ten years old, so she lived without a father present. My parents were constantly arguing, disagreeing about almost everything in life. They should have separated, but for whatever reason, never mustered the courage to take action. The fights between them were nasty and vitriolic, and seemingly constant, not making a welcoming environment for anyone.

"Why did they get married in the first place?"

"What mistakes they all made."

"Didn't they ever discuss their values, desires, hopes, dreams? What did they want out of life?"

Sheila and I talked into the late-night exploring these issues.

I had professed my love for her and her for me. We were infatuated, certainly in a physical way, but more importantly with each other as people. Our personalities were compatible. Our likes and dislikes quite similar, and our values encompassing our outlook on life meshed perfectly. Our goals, hopes, dreams were nearly the same. We both wanted to share this wonderful harmony in a marriage of kindred spirits.

But we were hesitant given the experiences of our parents, and we both needed to explore everything about life's failures and successes during our late-night talks. Approaching this with gusto, our conversations were animated and sometimes loud. Yet, indicative of our relationship, our warm feelings and love for each other dominated our courtship. Where others hopelessly tumbled toward marriage, we proceeded in a more measured strategic fashion, yet no less madly in love. Sheila and I were, and always would be a team, a single functioning unit joined in happiness and gentle caring.

She was already working as a dental hygienist when I graduated college. Soon after I received my degree, we married blissfully, moving into adult life, testing our beliefs and values together.

CHAPTER 7 -- CONNECTICUT

"Hey Ken, would you be interested in moving to Connecticut?" said the voice on the other side of the phone. "I've just been promoted to a new position. We've reorganized the department and need someone with your set of skills and experience. Naturally, we'll recognize your talent with a higher salary. Do you have any interest? If you do, I'll tell you more about it, and then you can take a trip up here and interview with the Vice President and Senior Vice President."

"It sounds very appealing. Of course, I need to speak with my wife and find out if she would consider relocating. We haven't been here that long, and we really like where we live."

Two months later, Sheila and I moved to a lovely townhouse, renting it from the owners. It was part of a condominium complex, larger than the apartment we lived in before. Earning more money in the new job, Sheila and I were proud of our higher standard of living. It was quite a jump for two kids from relatively poor parents growing up in Brooklyn, New York, in the 1950s and 1960s.

"You sure are our good luck charm." Sheila kissed Kim on the forehead as she took her afternoon nap. Things were moving along just right for the three of us.

While we both were reaping the rewards of middle-class life as new parents, Sheila and I began to discuss the possibilities of expanding our family. We had always wanted four kids, and that desire was rekindled by the great delight we received from Kim.

"Caring for Kim, enjoying every second with her, makes me realize how much I enjoy bringing up children. How much I enjoy being a mother. And how much I want a larger family," Sheila reflected.

"I just want more kids to care for, to hug, to kiss, and to play with. I want to watch them grow, moving through each stage. As an infant, baby, toddler. I've loved it all, and I am looking forward to the times when Kim is in kindergarten, although I know I'll be sad when I'm no longer with her all day."

"Then she'll be in grade school, high school, and beyond. Wouldn't it be wonderful if there were younger ones passing through the earlier stages at the same time? I really think that being a parent adds completeness to your life."

"Yeah," I agreed. "It's all about caring and loving another person and then watching them slowly grow up. And at the same time, you mature and develop as a human being through the experience. I can't think of anything in life more rewarding."

"Of course, we both recognize we're fortunate to feel the same way. There are many people that don't necessarily see it quite the way we do. Not as strongly, anyway." We had discussed these things so many times before we were married that we knew we were in sync.

Sheila and I engaged in similar discussions over the next few months. But there was the elephant in the room, hiding behind the drapes.

"We both agree that we want, no, need, a larger family. We love kids. But what about the past and what does it mean for the future? Do we move ahead, or are remembrances going to make us reluctant? And how do we proceed? Do we adopt again or try to have a biological child? Based on our experience, each of these paths can be muddied or even impossible, blocked by many dangerous crossroads."

Sheila summed up our dilemma exactly with her spot-on rhetorical questions.

"I sure don't know at this point," I explained, "but let's keep talking and turning the apple around to see it from all angles, and maybe we'll find the right answers. That's what we usually do."

"Yes, we do," Sheila agreed. "And it usually seems to work."

Two months later, Sheila visited her OB-GYN for a regular check-up and returned with some good news.

"Dr. Harris told me about a new medical procedure that can determine in utero if a baby's lungs are mature and ready to breathe on their own. Remember hyaline membrane disease that Matthew died from?" Basically, he died because his lungs were not matured.

"Of course I do."

"Well, the doctor described that in the past it was a guessing game to determine when the baby's lungs were ready, particularly when to perform a C-section. It was based on physical examination and the estimate of exactly how far along you were in the last months of the pregnancy. Both were imprecise.

"That's what the doctors had explained to us after Matthew's death. It's what we understood to be the case. We were assured by everyone from OB-GYNs to our GP to the genetics expert we talked to again that our two babies died from completely unrelated causes. One had nothing at all to do with the other. The only caveat to some degree was that the first baby was indirectly responsible for the death of the second baby because I needed a second C-section after the size of Carolyn's head made the first one necessary. And it was the guessing game about Matthew's lungs that missed, resulting in the hyaline membrane disease that killed him."

"Sure, I remember all this. We discussed it a few times before dropping it. We hit the odds of about one in one hundred thousand both times, one of the doctors told us. Completely separate and unrelated causes."

"Well, Dr. Harris says that there's a new test out that can very precisely determine the maturity of a baby's lungs. It's called amniocentesis. They actually stick a needle in the amniotic fluid and extract some. Then they can tell from the chemicals present in the fluid. Isn't that great?" Sheila related this good news with a guarded smile breaking out on her face.

"It sure is," I responded.

"That means we can rule out the cause of Matthew's death if we try for a biological child. Then there's the hydrocephalus that led to Carolyn's death. And we know that it probably wasn't a genetic issue inherited from us. That means we would enter any pregnancy with the one in one hundred thousand chance that everyone else faces.

"So maybe the new test is telling us that trying another time for a biological child is the way to go," Sheila reasoned.

"I suppose so," I agreed.

We were grateful to be armed with this encouraging information. Still, we wanted to limit our all-encompassing desire for more children from developing into a quixotic approach to the future. Attempting to marginalize our feelings and emotions, Sheila and I agreed we needed to move forward guided by well-informed and reasoned decisions.

*****

"I'm pregnant," Sheila declared when I opened the door, just arriving home from work. I dropped my attaché case and gave her a big hug and kiss. Kim, who was now about two and a half years old, wrapped her arms around our legs as we stood in the doorway in a close embrace.

We had carefully considered all the information we could amass. Cautiously optimistic based on all the advice we had received over the past months, Sheila and I couldn't be more pleased.

"My mother and sister have encouraged me to deliver in

Manhattan this time, where they think the best care is available. So I'm going to see an OB-GYN in Stamford who is associated with a large New York hospital. It's about an hour drive from here to his office, but that's not a problem," Sheila told me.

"I don't know if that makes sense. But, if you think it's for the best, that's your decision to make. Of course, I'll support whatever you decide to do."

"Good." Sheila spoke in a soft voice as she stepped closer to kiss me.

Three months later, Sheila informed me emphatically, "I'm changing doctors and hospitals."

"Oh," I said, surprised at her words.

"Driving to Stamford today, I fell asleep at the wheel. Just for a moment, but I almost veered off the highway at sixty miles an hour. I woke with a start, petrified, my heart pounding while I pulled over to the side of the road.

"I've been questioning the decision in my own mind for a few weeks now. After this incident on the highway, I realized then that New York was the wrong decision. We know that Yale New Haven Hospital is a high quality regional medical center much closer to our house. So when I told the doctor in Stamford about the scare I just had driving to his office, I asked him what he thought.

"He let me know, 'I was waiting for you to ask. What took you so long? Yale New Haven Hospital is world-renowned, and I believe should be a short fifteen- to twenty-minute drive from where you live. It only makes sense that you should be seen by a doctor associated with Yale and deliver at their hospital. They are one of the best, if not the best."

"He gave me the name of a doctor, a professor at the Yale Medical School, and I've already called and scheduled an appointment."

"That sounds like the correct decision to me for all the right reasons. You knew I questioned whether delivering in Manhattan was appropriate. I just wasn't sure if the logic behind that decision held up. But how about your mother and sister? They were so adamant about New York."

"Well, I've already spoken to both of them. They strongly resisted my decision initially. I sure didn't want to alienate them. We don't need a strained relationship with them. They kept pressing me on the phone. I stopped them and told them that this decision is one I have already made, and it's very important to me that I have their total support. Fortunately, those words had a lot of persuasive power. Telling them that the doctor in Stamford also suggested Yale New Haven Hospital was the icing on the cake."

"So that's all settled?" I asked.

"Right now, and hopefully for the duration."

"Great. And a really good decision," I declared.

*****

"Do you feel the baby?" Sheila asked, holding Kim's hand on her swollen belly.

"Yes."

"Do you feel the baby moving?"

Kim nodded with a smile.

"Was I in your belly, too, Mommy?" she asked Sheila with her hand still in place.

"Not really, Kim. You were in another woman's belly. That woman couldn't take care of you, so she let me be your mommy. She was very kind to do that. And you are so very special. Daddy and I are the luckiest people in the world to have you as our daughter. We love you so very much."

"I love you, too, Mommy." Kim hugged Sheila around the hips where she stood.

"Oh, that feels so good," Sheila shook back and forth with delight and kissed Kim on the top of her head.

"We're so lucky to be a family and have each other. And soon you'll have a baby sister or brother. We will all love each other so very much."

"Good things are on the march," I said after returning home

from work that same evening and Sheila relayed her discussion with Kim verbatim. I was holding her in my arms as I did every night, and I kissed her on the cheek as I squeezed her tightly. Her warm body felt so good in my arms. We were a happy family and soon would be an even larger happy family.

"You know, Yale New Haven is just a great place," Sheila told me after Kim went to bed and the two of us were alone. "Dr. Dawes is a great guy. He's very knowledgeable. And the facility is first-rate. You know that those first two ultrasounds of the baby showed he was fine.

"It's an amazing scientific development. They're not only able to see his outline in the womb, but they were able to tell he's a boy. It's just fantastic to see those black and white outlines of him. I know that Yale is spearheading the development of fetal ultrasound and its various applications. We're in the right place for sure."

We both felt quite confident with the care Sheila and our baby were receiving. Yale was a terrific place and the cause for our guarded optimism.

*****

"I have some difficult news for both of you," Dr. Dawes said as Sheila and I sat in his modestly furnished office. Our hearts sank at hearing these words. "Today's ultrasound showed some anomalies with the past ones and with expected norms. Your son's head seems out of proportion to his torso and limbs. Unfortunately, that would suggest the possibility of hydrocephalus, the same affliction suffered by your first baby. It's a bit early to be absolutely certain. I thought of waiting a few weeks after our next ultrasound to avoid alarming you, but I wanted to be totally straight with you and give you all the information that I have, bad or good."

The news hit us like the blast from a furnace.

My first reaction was to curse under my breath in frustration and dismay.

"Like our first baby?" Sheila shuddered as she repeated the doctor's words.

"Yes. But again, we have to wait two weeks to be absolutely positive. I know that it won't be an easy time for you given your past experience. But I've gotten to know you two, and if anyone can get through this period whole, it's you."

The doctor's kind words were designed to help, but we barely heard them. We were in a fog, crushed by the news, and not able to think clearly, if at all. Emotions welled inside us. We were badly shaken, brought to our knees by this totally unexpected information.

"How do we get through this?" Sheila wondered as we sat in a restaurant near our home. Frozen, we didn't move. We tried in vain to absorb what Dr. Dawes had told us. We were drowning in an ocean of sadness and fear.

Sheila and I didn't know what to do with ourselves, and we didn't want our daughter to see how devastated we were. So we called my mother who was watching Kim and told her something had come up that we needed to do. We wouldn't be home for a few hours more.

"That's good," she said. "It just gives me more time to play with my granddaughter. I'll enjoy every minute of it. Take your time and do whatever you have to do. Don't rush home. I'm fine."

"I can't eat a thing," Sheila murmured after our food was brought by a jovial waiter.

"Me neither." I pushed my plate to the side of the table.

"Why did we come here anyway?" Sheila asked.

"Who knows," I babbled.

"This is madness."

We looked at each other through a gauzy haze.

Sitting for a while, just staring in space, neither of us was able to speak. The silence was palpable. Our minds were racing with incoherence. The terrible news plunged us into despair. It seemed profane. We were left with but a tenuous hold on reality as we sank into oblivion, frozen and motionless.

"Anything wrong with your food?" the waiter asked when

he passed our table and noticed the full plates pushed to the side.

"No," I responded curtly. "Just please bring us the check."

"That's okay, right? That we leave now."

"Sure," Sheila whispered weakly. "I don't know. I'm so confused. I don't know where we should be or what we should be doing. I'm lost."

"Me, too."

About half an hour later we arrived back at the townhouse we were renting. Opening the door, we entered like two nomads wandering in the wilderness, blank expressions on our faces.

"So, how did it go?" my mother asked carefully, sensing the state we were in.

She realized that the news from the ultrasound test may not have been good, or that something else went awry. Her question seemed to fade into the air, diffusing as it rose to the ceiling.

"I put Kim in for a nap just before you came home," she said after a minute of silence. She didn't know what else to say.

We still didn't respond.

I tried to gather my wits, but couldn't, my mind in a dense cloud of distress, shrouded in misery. Then realizing I couldn't be silent forever, I spoke in a halting voice. My mother listened intently.

"It's not good," I told her. I spoke first in order to spare Sheila from repeating the dreadful information. "The baby may be developing the same thing that our first baby had," I informed my mother in a broken voice, swallowing the lumps that kept developing in my throat. My face covered by a wet film of sweat, I was ashen underneath. When the words left my lips, my mouth swelled. I breathed heavily and erratically. I felt like my heart had stopped beating.

My mother fell into the couch, slumped over, her quivering hands covering her face. She looked at the floor and clutched her breast like someone who had been shot by an assassin. There was no blood, but she was drenched in horror. The gut-wrenching news sent her reeling, like a boxer to the canvas.

"No, no," was all she could say.

Sheila was still standing by my side, wobbly but erect. She began to sob after she heard the awful news for the second time. She was trembling.

When my mother saw Sheila crying, she slowly raised herself from the couch on shaky legs and grabbed Sheila in a warm embrace. They both sank back down holding each other tightly. They wept together in each other's arms, suffocating with grief.

Sheila tried to speak in order to thank my mother for her caring, but her breath had obviously been choked from her lungs. She said later she felt as if she was being strangled.

I collapsed in the large chair next to the couch.

How could this happen? I thought. *Why should my wonderful wife be tormented this way?*

Very quickly, my mind began to drift as before, wandering off course. I was headed to nowhere. It flashed back to the total state of confusion and incoherence. The contours of the living room seemed to waver as I lost my grip on reality again. The air felt thick and heavy.

The three of us remained as we were for what seemed an eternity. An hour passed. Then, showing her usual strength, Sheila sat up erect on the couch, dried her eyes, and began to speak. Clearly, she had regained her composure. My mother and I were still in shock, but seeing Sheila recovered, ready to say something, felt like we were brushed by an angel's wings. That soft mild feeling somehow lifted the fog from our minds. The dense turbulent mist of confusion began to clear.

"Well, we three are a sight to behold. Now that we've had a good cry, we need to get on with life. True, we're rattled and shaken. But there's hope as Dr. Dawes explained that things can work out, that our son might be healthy," Sheila pronounced. "So we need to stop lamenting what hasn't happened yet. We need to move on, if not for ourselves, then for Kim. We can't let her see how upset we are. We need to be strong for her and ourselves."

It was clear that Sheila was not going to surrender to misery and self-pity. "It was good that we allowed ourselves to collapse in pain. That was a necessary catharsis. Now we need to recover from our initial emotions and start looking positively to the future. We can't be angry or feel sorry for ourselves.

"I know that we're dreadfully upset, punched in the stomach by the news. But we need to focus on the possible positive outcome two weeks from now. We need to keep our heads up, show some courage or these next two weeks will be a living hell. It'll kill all three of us. And I won't be a part of that." Sheila scoffed at the ideas of self-pity and crippling frustration, which would only result in more misery. She refused to surrender to doubt and negative thoughts.

My wife was held in high regard, respect, and affection by everyone who knew her. Sheila's stalwart character was admired and praised, serving as a model for resiliency and endurance. She was a paragon of courage. These traits were balanced by her kindness and caring for others. She was nice to everyone, and her delicate sweetness belied the toughness inside. When she spoke, people listened; her soft but trenchant words were not wasted on me and my mother.

I knew I had to equal her strength.

"Of course you're right," I said, rising from my chair.

"You're amazing. Damn, do I love you." I kissed her on the lips. They were cold and dry, still recovering from the ominous news.

"We'll get through this like we have every other nasty thing that's happened in the past," Sheila concluded.

"You said we need to be strong for Kim," I added, "and we do. I think we also need to be optimistic for Carolyn and Matthew. We owe it to them, so their deaths might have some meaning."

Sheila's approach to this situation was rubbing off on me. From her stamina and spirit, I had gained the energy to push forward many times in the past. This was no exception. She would only view the future with contagious optimism, preventing us from drowning in sorrow or despair.

Listening to us, my mother rebounded after a while. Although still distraught, she was now encouraged by Sheila's positive tone.

"Let's wash the tears off our faces. Kim will be getting up soon," she said.

*****

"Sorry to have heard the news, Ken," the vice president of my department at work offered his sympathy for my situation. I had taken two days off, one for the ultrasound test and the next to regain my stability and composure.

"You know we're all here to help in any way we can. I want you to know that you should feel free to take any time you need away from this department. Come and go as you please. I know you're working on some critical projects, but they can wait in a situation like this. Now is your time and you need to use it as you see fit.

"Now I have to go to an important meeting. Good luck, and please keep us posted on any developments if you can find the time."

With that, he stood to exit his lavish office, leaving me sitting in one of the chairs facing his desk.

"Thanks so much, Bob, so very much for your support of my wife and me. I really do appreciate it."

"Don't mention it," he responded sincerely. "It's the least we can do. So get on with your life and face this crisis as best you can. We're here for you."

Bob disappeared out his office door, heading down the corridor leading to the executive conference room.

I got up slowly from my chair. My eyes were a bit watery with the feeling that I wasn't alone. With a slight sense of relief, I returned downstairs to my work area.

I informed Sheila of my meeting as soon as I returned home

from work that evening.

"Bob is just great, and the company is behind us. They'll support us in any way possible."

She smiled at me.

"See, I always tell you there are kind and caring folks in this world, many more than your cynical, skeptical self believes. But I know that eventually, you do come around."

"As usual you're right," I agreed. "I only come around because I listen to you, babe."

CHAPTER 8 -- TWO WEEKS

Sheila tried to bathe the next two weeks in her eternal optimism. She was successful to a degree. At times, when the free-flowing hope from her spring of promise wavered in the face of reality, we could get down for a while. There were agonizing moments for both of us.

Nights were marked by fitful sleep and troubled dreams. Our bedroom appeared to develop shadowy crevices. Its edges seemed to change. The walls appeared to be closing in on us. In one instance, Sheila awoke with a start at about three in the morning. She was shaking, her heart was pounding, and she was covered in a cold sweat.

"I saw the silhouette of a dying baby against the window," she whispered to me as I jumped up from my unsettled rest. "It was convulsing in agony."

"It was just another bad dream." I rolled over to her side of the bed and held her tightly in my arms.

"I know. But they're so awful and scary." She shivered. "Please don't stop. Hold me forever."

"Sure. But it'll be awkward at work," I joked, trying to lighten the moment.

"I love you," she said. "Just don't let go."

"After all we've endured, it sure feels unfair that we find ourselves in this situation," I observed after a while. "But given all the barriers we've overcome, maybe this is just another roadblock in our way. And this time, just a temporary one."

We remained in each other's comforting arms until we heard Kim stirring in the bedroom. Neither of us had fallen back to sleep.

Frequently during the two weeks, bad thoughts tormented my mind. I wondered whether Kim was only a brief respite from the dirge of our past. Had our ecstasy been brief? Cut off before it would blossom? Was our passionate desire to cling to another being as beautiful as Kim to be denied? Was our hope just a veneer, or did we really bemoan our harrowing misfortune, betrayed yet again by fate, even mocked by it? Did we need to recalibrate our world as we wrestled with what might be? I wasn't sure of anything.

*****

"There's nothing wrong, I'm pretty sure. Look how I'm carrying. It's very different than with Carolyn, and I'm feeling active life. You do, too, when you hold your hand on my belly." Sheila repeated these words on many days, sometimes sounding like she was trying to convince herself.

I dragged through the next two weeks, buoyed only by my lovely wife's hope. I was fraying at the edges. She was a pillar of strength, although inside I knew she had her doubts and fears. Tired lines developed on our faces from worry and lack of sleep. Words of encouragement from family and friends were welcome but had their limits. We hoped for the best but braced ourselves for the worst.

*****

"It seems to be taking forever," Sheila's voice was weak and a bit scared.

"Maybe the longer it takes, the better the news," I mused.

"You know that I'm not carrying as big as with Carolyn. You see it and I feel it. It's like Matthew who had no problems with hydrocephalus. I'm really confident that things are okay."

Sheila was sincere in her words as usual, but now that we had waited for more than a half-hour, a hint of doubt crept in, coloring her speech.

We were sitting nervously in Dr. Dawes' office at the end of the designated two-week period. Sheila had just had an internal examination and ultrasound test. With no definitive answer, we were on edge, to say the least.

"Everything looks fine," Dr. Dawes announced with a large smile on his face. He touched both of us on the shoulder, confirming the good news as he entered his office.

"Your internal and the ultrasound results indicate that you're further along in your pregnancy than we expected based on the information you had given us about your menstrual cycle. So the baby's cranium is within normal limits. Also, when you began to see me, I had explained that we are a pioneering institution in using ultrasound for intrauterine determinations. Dr. McDougle came from Edinburgh in Scotland to head up our efforts. He's world-renowned for his research and expertise. But since the test has only been used for a few years and in limited medical facilities, the normative data aren't perfect. All we could do in the prior ultrasound was to compare your baby's size and development with the existing data. It appeared by that standard, that your son's head size was beyond statistical norms. Of course, we may have been influenced to some degree by the condition of your first hydrocephalic child."

We sat listening without a word.

"It's unfortunate you had to be exposed to an anxiety-provoking two-week waiting period. But based on today's tests, I think you're in the clear and can look forward to a healthy baby.

"And the other reason why I say this is because of the test I explained to you before, amniocentesis. To reiterate, we place a needle into the amniotic fluid and withdraw a small amount. By testing the chemicals in the fluid, we can determine if the baby's lungs are mature enough to function on their own outside of your body. Unlike the ultrasound, this is a precise chemical analysis, no judgment involved. I'll perform the procedure every two weeks from now on and we will avoid anything like what happened to your second baby, hyaline membrane disease. So I think from now on we're on safe ground. We can expect smooth sailing ahead."

Sheila and I sat motionless for a few moments. Then, as the wonderful news sunk in, we both smiled after a tremendous sigh of relief. Sheila was the first to speak.

"Thank you, Doctor. This certainly is really good news. I always say; it doesn't matter if the rehearsal didn't go well as long as opening night is a success."

"That's a fine way to look at it," said Dr. Dawes.

"And this is a great opening night," I added.

We left the doctor's office and jumped into each other's arms with ecstasy. It appeared that our dreams of having more than one child would be realized. A girl and a boy. We were excited beyond words.

"Fantastic," my mother said, who had been babysitting Kim. She grabbed me by the waist and nearly squeezed the air out of my lungs with the biggest hug ever. Then she kissed Sheila on the cheek.

"The two of you deserve this, deserve this so much," she concluded warmly. "I'm so happy for you."

We were so very excited. Still, because of our past, we were compelled to steel ourselves against the advent of some unforeseen problem developing over the next few weeks. While fortifying ourselves against any possibility, we tried not to allow caution to detract from our joy and positive expectations.

"It's going to be fine now. Everything will work out," Sheila said with just the slightest tinge of hesitancy in her voice.

*****

"The amniocentesis shows that your baby's lungs are already operating independently," Dr. Dawes informed us. "So on the way out, stop at the desk and schedule your C-section for some time early next week. I'll let the nurse know, and I'll see you next in the hospital. Before you two leave, I want to discuss another issue with you."

These words caused an expression of deep concern to cover our faces. Dr. Dawes recognized this immediately. "Please don't be concerned. I'm sorry I may have scared you. There's nothing wrong, I assure you.

"I just wanted to discuss the issue of the size of your family now and the potential risks for C-sections beyond the one you're about to have. Our experience shows that each C-section brings with it potential complications for the mother; the possibility of the rupture of her uterus. This will be your third C-section, and after that, the risks rise substantially. The fourth carries much more jeopardy for the mother than the third.

"In addition, you will have a girl and a boy, a lovely family by any measure. So putting the two together, I feel it's my responsibility to suggest you consider having a tubal ligation, commonly called having your tubes tied. This will prevent any possibility of another pregnancy and the associated risk to Sheila. I think you should give this serious consideration.

"Of course, it needs to be a decision you're completely comfortable with. If you can decide, let me know before we perform your C-section so that I can do the procedure then. That makes sense since your fallopian tubes will be exposed to us, and we can avoid another operative procedure with the normal attendant risk, discomfort, and inconvenience to say the least.

"I know that was a mouthful and a lot to seriously consider in a relatively short period of time. But I would be remiss as a medical professional not to present it to you. So please think about it and let me know as soon as you can."

"We understand," I said. "Thank you, Doctor."

Sheila and I left the office after scheduling the C-section.

"Well, that gives us just a few days to decide." We were in

our car, and I already reached my conclusion about the tubal ligation.

"Here's where I am," I told Sheila. "I agree with the doctor's reasoning. He's certain this baby will be fine, and that gives us a girl and a boy. I see that side of it. The most important thing for me, though, is your health. I don't want to see you put at risk, for your sake of course, but also for mine. You and Kim are the most important people in the world to me. I can't live without you. You are my love and my sustenance. I would never expose you to any unnecessary risk. That's it, that's where I am. I don't need to think about it anymore."

"I love you, Ken. And I suppose I'm in the same place you are. I owe it to you and Kim not to expose myself to anything risky. Still, let's take a few days to mull it over to be absolutely sure about anything sounding so final, so irreversible."

"How can I disagree with that?" I said. "We'll take a few days to discuss it more and then we'll let Dr. Dawes know our decision."

*****

"Wow, he's just great," I told Sheila as I leaned over her hospital bed to kiss her on the forehead. She was in pain from the C-section incision, but this time happiness enveloped her, diminishing any discomfort.

"I was able to suit up in whites and special sanitized gloves. In these, I can enter the Infant Intensive Care Unit. I've held his hand and touched his face through special holes in the side of his clear plastic covered crib. Dr. Dawes says Daniel is doing great and you should be able to hold him tomorrow when they release him from the unit."

"I know having him down there is just a precaution because of our past history. Dr. Dawes didn't want to take any chances. I'm so happy and at peace, but I long to see and hold him. Well, in another day I will."

Just then Dr. Dawes entered Sheila's room.

"Your son is doing quite well, which I'm sure Ken's told you already. You're so comfortable down in the unit, you look like one of the staff," he joked, looking directly at me.

Then he looked back at Sheila. "Your C-section went fine. Given some of the advances we've made in the surgery, you may be discharged in just a few days, rather than the week required when you had your last one three years ago.

"And we performed the tubal ligation as you had desired. It also went quite well. As a medical doctor, I'm really pleased that the two of you made the decision to have the procedure. It just makes sense. Now please forgive me for the very brief visit, but I have other patients to see. Congratulations again."

The next day, when I entered Sheila's room, she was holding Daniel, the name we had decided to give our son.

"I didn't think he'd be out of the Infant Intensive Care Unit so quickly," Sheila said. "A nurse brought him to me about an hour or so ago. I can feel the immediate bonding with him. He's so peaceful. It's so special having him next to me. It's just wonderful. I'm in heaven."

The next few days, I visited Sheila as often as possible.

Free of concerns, Sheila had thrown herself into holding and feeding Daniel, the brightness of her eyes lighting up the room. I lingered at her bedside, filled with happiness, not wanting to leave my wife and our new son.

"You know that you're beaming, just the way you looked after we adopted Kim. I can see that you're at peace. Your radiance is just so beautiful."

"Thanks," she said, blushing. "I am at peace. That word, 'son,' sure sounds wonderful when you say it. Speaking of Kim, how is my lovely daughter? As much as I'm floating on a cloud when I hold Daniel, I really miss that gal of mine. Her blonde hair, her voice, and her smile."

"She's doing fine but missing you, too. Soon you'll be together again, and now she has a brother, too."

When I drove Sheila and Daniel home from the hospital, the azure sky was lit by a brilliant, smiling sun. Good fortune had prevailed. We just knew the powerful headwinds battering our lives had abated. The storms of fate were gone forever.

A week passed. Sheila was home only two days and had already organized a celebration at our house. Some of our close relatives and friends helped in the bustle to prepare the party.

Our townhouse was overflowing with happy, enthusiastic people. Decorations and balloons adorned every corner of the living area. A dazzling array of gifts clogged the kitchen.

The party was a bit subdued for a short half an hour, and then a noisy celebration spontaneously broke out. Fueled by good food and drink, there was a frenzy of hugs, kisses, and well-wishing. The loud conversations and laughter escalated to a fever pitch.

Many of our guests approached us, sharing heartfelt words and warm embraces.

"Congratulations, good luck."

"We're so happy for you. We expect only the best for both of you in the future."

"You guys rule." Then looking only at Sheila, they said, "You rock, girl."

"You deserve all this happiness after all you've gone through. Congratulations."

"We wish you all the best with your new family. We're so happy for you."

"It's a delight to share this moment with the two of you. All the best."

"What a pleasure to be here with you in this hour of joy. Our warmest congratulations."

As the merrymaking continued, the time arrived for me to deliver a speech I had prepared for the occasion.

"May I have your attention, please," I requested in a loud voice. "Please may I have your attention for just a few minutes." It was necessary to repeat myself a few more times before the noise in the room dwindled, finally settling in quiet.

"I know you've all been fortified by the delicious food my wife prepared, not to mention the continuous flow of alcohol."

"Yaaay," yelled a few of the male guests who were clearly enjoying themselves.

"Welcome. I'd like to thank you for being here today to celebrate the birth of our son, Daniel. Sheila and I are delighted you're here to share in our joy. Family, friends, and neighbors, I hope you're having a wonderful time."

Again, the air was filled with loud hoots and hollers.

"I do, however, want to interrupt the festivities for a few minutes. I think it's appropriate for me to say a few words expressing our gratitude for the gift Sheila and I have been given. Some of you know pieces of our story, some are aware of small parts, while a few of you know very little. Only a handful of you know it all. So I thought I would summarize our journey to becoming parents so you can truly understand the great depth of our appreciation and joy.

"As many of you know, Sheila and I have not had an easy time, to say the least, when it comes to having children."

A pervasive silence filled the room as I began.

"First, there was Carolyn who died at birth from hydrocephalus. The fluid drowning her brain had stopped most bodily functions. We mourned Carolyn, our firstborn, but gaining strength from each other, we looked to the future. Genetic counseling showed no predisposition toward Carolyn's affliction, so we tried again.

"Matthew, our second, was delivered prior to the maturation of his lungs, leading to a condition known as hyaline membrane disease or HMD, which is often fatal. In essence, the baby is deprived of oxygen and then succumbs.

"It was discovered that Matthew, who was delivered a little over a year after Carolyn's demise, had developed HMD in his second day of life. He was rushed from the hospital in which he was born to one that had special expertise and equipment to care for HMD babies. To our dismay and horror, his lungs had deteriorated beyond help when he arrived at the new facility. Standing helplessly by, I held his tiny hand as I watched him die. That sight haunts me still today.

"Sheila and I had a rough, challenging time after Matthew's passing. We had thought we were parents, but that characterization only lasted less than forty-eight hours."

Reaching this section of my speech, it was quite difficult for me to breathe normally and not sob. Words stuck in my throat, and I had to stop for a moment to gather myself. During this pause, I could hear quite a few of our guests beginning to weep, some even cry. I continued on when I was able to breathe normally again.

"After our second tragedy, Sheila and I decided to adopt a child. We were frustrated, discouraged, and disappointed after approaching adoption agencies, none of which would help us for various reasons. Then, with help from my brother Phil, Kim came into our lives through a process called a private adoption under New York State law. And there she is, bouncing on my father's knee." I pointed to the couch where my father was sitting.

"Hi Kim, I love you," I said, waving my hand in her direction.

"Hi Daddy, I love you, too." Kim's response broke the heaviness in the room for a brief moment as many chuckles lightened the air. Some of those who were crying briefly smiled.

"Kim helped save us from sinking into the depths of despair. She was our salvation at the time. She is our joy, our good luck charm.

"When our golden girl was two, we decided to try again to have a biological child, a brother or sister for Kim. In Sheila's eighth month of pregnancy, our doctors thought this baby was developing hydrocephalus, like Carolyn, our first. They told us that a two-week period was needed to be certain. That time placed a tremendous strain on both of us as we grappled with all possibilities. After a two-week waiting period, during which Sheila and I went through a living hell, a new medical test lifted the cloud of gloom.

"And now, here is our new gift, Daniel, whose birth completes our life's mosaic. We're so very fortunate to have him. We just couldn't be more thrilled. After all the adversity we faced together, Sheila and I now have a girl and a boy, a complete and wonderful family. We're elated, overwhelmed with joy."

As I looked around, I saw people weeping, crying, and sobbing. I don't think there was a dry eye in our house. Wonderfully, tears of sadness had now been transformed into tears of joy and good cheer as smiles reappeared in the room.

"Please let me thank those of you here today who helped us with support and caring through these past five years. Your love and friendship mean a great deal to us. Thank you so much. I'd like to end by thanking my wife. Her mettle, strength of character, and her resiliency are the reason we're here today. Her love has gotten me through this. I owe this all to her." A wild cheer erupted that shook our townhouse walls. Sheila was teary-eyed as person after person hugged her with joyous arms.

"Now!" I yelled as loud as I could, attempting to gain the crowd's attention again.

"My younger brother, Mark, has told me he has something special for all of us."

Mark stood next to me and announced, "This is a song I picked for this occasion. I hope you all enjoy it. The words aren't perfect. Their context and reference are different from what this party is celebrating, but the name and many of the lines ring true."

He spoke in a raspy voice since he had been cheering and applauding before and after my speech.

With that short introduction, Mark pivoted, walked to our hi-fi, and placed a forty-five record on the turntable. The guests became quiet again as a soothing melody began.

The room was filled with the sound of "Daniel" by Sir Elton John. "Daniel is traveling tonight on a plane…" As the recording continued, two lines struck all of us, capturing our emotions. Again, reddened cheeks grew wet with tears, tears of gladness.

"God it looks like Daniel must be the clouds in my eyes," and especially, "Daniel you're a star in the face of the sky."

When the song ended, an uproarious round of applause, accompanied by shouting and yelling, spread throughout our townhouse. The windows seemed to rattle, and the walls rumbled as the noise continued. Exuberant expressions of congratulations and well-wishes overflowed as the revelry continued.

After many hours, our guests began to leave. Sheila and I thanked them for coming and being part of our celebration for Daniel. Each goodbye ended with a warm hug and many kisses.

We were disappointed when the last person left. The merriment had warmed our hearts. But we couldn't have been happier with the sunshine that was brightening our lives.

"You two must be exhausted," my mother said as she embraced both of us. "I'll put Kim into bed after you say goodnight to her. Then you can relax, take it easy. Let's leave the cleanup for tomorrow. I'll help out in the morning."

"Thanks, Mom," Sheila responded warmly. "And thanks so much for offering to stay and help with the kids for the next week. Wow, those words sound great: the kids." Sheila beamed.

After sitting on our couch talking about the party, we headed upstairs and collapsed in our bed. We were smiling before we fell to sleep, satisfaction, and a sense of triumph glowing across our faces.

The days passed swiftly by until the next weekend arrived. Early Saturday morning, the doorbell rang unexpectedly. I walked to the door and opened it.

"Good morning, Ken."

Our next-door neighbor, Irene, offered a robust greeting.

"Hi. Good morning to you too."

"It's for you babe, Irene's here." I had turned, raising my voice so Sheila could hear me in the kitchen.

"I'm coming," she shouted back. "Tell Irene I'll be right

there."

"Hi Sheila," Irene said as my wife rushed to the opened door.

"Good morning. Won't you come in?" Sheila responded, stepping sideways and beckoning to Irene with her left hand.

"Thanks. But actually, I'm here to invite you over to our house for some coffee and conversation. A few of the other neighbors are coming over, and I thought you would like to join in."

"I'd love to. Just give me a few minutes to freshen up and tell Ken and his mom. She's here helping out."

"Yes, I know. And I think it's great that she's here. We all could see at the party how good she is with Kim, and how she jumps right in for all kinds of work."

"It's nice that you noticed. And the best part is that we get along so well. Ken's mom and I are very close. I cherish that relationship. Okay. I'll be right over."

"Great, I'll see you in a bit," said Irene as she took the short walk back to her house.

"I'm headed to Irene's. Don't know when I'll be back. Just some coffee with a few of the neighbors, so it shouldn't be more than two hours or so at the most," Sheila told my mother and me, heading out the door.

It took less than five minutes to get to Irene's house. When she returned home, Sheila told me that after she rang the bell, the door opened, and "Surprise!" rang out when she stepped into the living room.

Six of the other neighbors who were friendly with Sheila were gathered in the room stacked with boxes brightly wrapped in blue gift paper. Sheila then related the details of what happened next.

She was so touched, she was speechless. Her eyes became watery. Irene gently held her around the waist with one hand and the shoulder with the other, guiding her to sit down in a soft chair by the couch.

A large coffee urn was next to the chair. Delicious-looking pastry sat on large silver trays adorning the tables in the living room.

Sheila snuggled the pillows on each side of her.

"Thank you so much." Sheila looked around the room at her neighbors. "This was not at all necessary. I really do appreciate it."

"Well," began Irene. "None of us knew very much about your history of having children. A few of us were aware that you had some problems, but we had no idea of what you've been through. We all cried our eyes out when Ken told everyone the details at your party last weekend. We haven't stopped talking about it all week. You're a very strong and courageous person to have gone through what you did and come out whole. We couldn't help feeling that you deserved something a little special from us."

"You purchased your good fortune and happiness with the currency of misery and sorrow," Sheila said another neighbor declared eloquently. "You earned all the joy you now have, and we all sincerely hope you'll suffer no more.

"So here's a tissue to dry your eyes. Now let's enjoy the coffee and goodies. Then we'll share in the fun when you open the presents for Daniel."

Sheila said her face lit up. "I'd love some coffee right now," she said to Irene.

The next two hours were spent in light and caring conversation among friends. Uncovering what was inside of the beautiful blue boxes brought laughter, with each gift acknowledged by applause and cheers.

"Thanks again, so very much," Sheila said with a smile of gratitude. She left to return back to our house, accompanied by her bounty of gifts, as many as she could carry.

CHAPTER 9 -- MOVING ON

"Hey babe, you'll never guess what happened today." I quizzed Sheila with a note of excitement in my voice.

"I just can't imagine," she replied. "But you sure look happy."

"You remember Jim, the guy who almost hired me before I accepted my current job."

"Sure. You always spoke so highly of him."

"Well, he called me today. It seems he's in the Detroit area heading up two major departments at one of the largest corporate conglomerates in the country. He wants me to go out there and work for him."

Sheila's expression shifted to one of some concern at hearing the news.

"You know I support you in any decision you make about your career, especially because they've always turned out so well for both of us and now our family. Gosh, I love saying that word, 'family'."

"But we only recently moved here, and Connecticut is wonderful. Our friends and neighbors are so warm and nice. This townhouse is lovely, and we've just now made it our own with new decorating and furniture. Kim loves it here, having fun at the playground and splashing in the community pool. Danny is just leaving the newborn stage, and he seems so comfortable with the surroundings, as I am. And I know you also enjoy it here. They value and respect you at work and you're thriving in the new company environment, even though you have a long commute. I know that I-95 is a pain with its traffic jams and long lines at the tolls. Still, overall, this situation is just right for us."

Then she paused momentarily.

"I have no doubt you're going to answer me with all the logic and facts in the world, as usual. But I just thought I would express my initial gut reaction."

"You know I always want your opinion, whether it's from the gut or well thought out," I began. "But let me outline why I think we should consider Jim's offer.

"Without prioritizing or sequencing in any order, I'll go through the main reasons a move makes sense. Then you can see if your initial gut feeling changes in any way.

"First, the company is profitable and stable. It's huge globally, opening up many career opportunities. The job has more management responsibilities than I have currently, leading to a manager-level position quickly if I deliver the analyses and programs Jim is looking for. I'm pretty confident I can. Where I am now, there are a number of guys blocking my promotional opportunities simply because of the organization structure, which is not likely to change. It'll be quite a while before I can reach management level. I know Jim, and I'm sure I'll really like working for him and learning from him, growing in expertise. And when I shared it with Bob, you know, the VP of my current company, he was really impressed and said that although he doesn't want to lose me, it sounds like a great opportunity, so just go for it. The icing on the cake is economic. The company will move us, and the pay Jim has tossed out is nearly forty percent more than I'm making now, including a bonus. That's a lot of money. And houses are much more reasonable in the Detroit area than in Connecticut. We may well be able to fulfill one of our economic dreams, buying a home.

"I also feel strongly that we can have a great life around Detroit, too, just as we do here, even though we'll be further away from family. We may have to leave some relationships with neighbors and others, but developing new friends has never been a problem, especially for you. It's one of your great strengths, and we'll both grow in the process.

"I say let's fly out to Detroit where I'll have to meet again with Jim and some of the other players in the company. We can look around and evaluate the situation further. Then we can make an informed decision, one way or another."

"Wow, that's a lot to absorb," Sheila responded, the look of doubt lifting from her face. "What you've said makes so much sense, as usual. Everything you explained sounds so positive. But I still have the concerns I expressed before, especially about the kids. I don't want them to be exposed to any stress or problems unnecessarily. I need to protect them from any type of instability. And I know you feel the same way although you haven't said so."

"I sure do," I interrupted her. "We need to protect them at all costs. That goes without saying. But I think we can minimize any negatives for the kids while taking advantage of a fine opportunity."

Then Sheila continued. "Despite my reservations, I'm pretty sure we can have a great life near Detroit, just like here, and the kids will thrive there, too. So, as the idea sinks in, I agree. Let's get more information and then evaluate the whole situation with all the facts. I know Mom will be happy to watch the kids."

"And with time, everything looks a little different as things settle in our minds and we gain more perspective," I added.

*****

"It was so nice of Jim to invite us for dinner, and his wife is just as lovely and hospitable as can be." Sheila began reviewing our test run to Detroit. We were comfortably seated on a Boeing 737 on our way home to Connecticut.

"The suburbs of Detroit seem like fine places to raise a family. And, wow, we can actually afford a four-bedroom newly built colonial only about a twenty-minute drive from where your new office would be. The neighborhood was crawling with children playing in their backyards and along the sidewalks. Young families all around. I think Kim and Danny will love it there."

"So, am I hearing support for the move?"

"Right now, yes. But of course, it's all very fresh and with some time my opinion may shift a bit. Now it really feels like all systems go," Sheila said with a big smile and quiet laugh.

"Me too," I said. "Jim and I still have some minor details to work out, but nothing that I can see as a deal-breaker."

"That's all well and good," Sheila continued. "I had an interesting and exciting long weekend, but I couldn't stop thinking about our Kim and Danny. Wow, I miss them so. I just want to hug the both of them, my arms ache for them. I feel so comfortable with your mother watching them. I know they're crazy about her. But I can't adjust to not having them with me. I love those two so much that being apart is painful. I can't wait to get home and see them."

"I've had the same feelings on business trips away from you and the kids," I said, confirming Sheila's comments. "That sense of emptiness and yearning never seems to go away."

Sheila pecked me on the cheek and smiled warmly. We didn't say much for the rest of the flight. Exhausted from the long days of exploration, we closed our eyes and relaxed for the remainder of the trip home.

*****

"What's that unbelievably loud sound? The room is filling up with smoke!" Sheila exclaimed a bit frantically. "I'll go check on the kids in the bedroom. Please try and figure out what's causing all this."

As she quickly disappeared, I opened the oven somewhat carefully and breathed a sigh of relief. I noticed a large piece of meat roasting in a tray. The inside of the oven was smoking like it was on fire, but no flames were apparent, so I shut off the oven and the smoke began to subside.

Just then Sheila returned from the bedroom. "Everything is fine in there," she said. "The kids are resting peacefully."

"It was just the oven causing the smoke, and it set off the alarm. I'll bet that thing hasn't been cleaned in a year, and whatever was stuck to the bottom and sides was smoldering. You wouldn't have noticed that when you put up the roast. It's been fine since I shut off the oven."

"We're fortunate that's all it was," Sheila said with a big grin growing along her mouth. "What a scare. We'll be moving into our new home as soon as the builder finishes the final touches. Then we won't have to have any more of these moments in this hotel."

We began to laugh loudly, both from a sense of relief, but mostly over the ridiculousness of the situation.

*****

"Well," I said, breathing out strongly, "that's the last bolt. It's finally finished and it sure was a lot more work than I ever thought it would be."

I was standing in the backyard of our new home admiring my handiwork, a metal playset complete with slide, swings, horizontal ladder, and thick rope for climbing. Its green finish sparkled in the bright Michigan spring afternoon.

"You've been at it since early this morning, around six hours of hard work. But it certainly looks like it was worth the effort."

"Looks great, doesn't it, kids?" Sheila said to Kim and Danny who had been looking on while I finished assembling the playset.

They both giggled and ran toward the large structure, eager to begin what would be many hours of fun crawling, climbing, and swinging.

"Whoa," I called out, causing both kids to stop in their tracks. I grabbed them both together and hugged them tightly.

"I need to test it first to see if it's sturdy and stable. And Mom and I need to tell you how to use it safely, like not walking behind or in front of anyone on the swings. Right, Mom?"

"Yep," Sheila said, and began the standard parents' instructional on safety and fun. She spent about half an hour explaining and demonstrating, and then the kids jumped on the swings.

"Damn, that was hard work," I said to Sheila, with my arm wrapped around her waist while we watched the kids frolicking on the playset. Danny was struggling somewhat as he was still a bit too small and not yet coordinated enough to engage in all the activities the set had to offer. Consistent with our child-rearing process, we let him find his own way while we helped a little.

"You know, that was a great feeling all morning and into the afternoon, putting the set together. Just another reaffirmation of me being a father, a dad to two wonderful kids. Even though it's been a few years, that feeling never seems to wear off with every new event and activity. I relish it, and most of all, I adore sharing it with you."

"You know I feel the same way," Sheila remarked.

"Every day is a joy," she continued as she carefully watched the kids playing. "Caring for those two, nurturing them, watching them grow is the greatest gift in my life. Kim is so physically skilled in every way, it's a wonder to watch her in action. She's capable of so much even at her age. And Danny is right behind her, although not as tall and strong. His verbal ability is amazing. What other two-year-old can have a flowing conversation with you and express himself so clearly? Best of all, the two of them play so well together. Sister and brother. What a treat to say those words."

"You bet," I said, reaffirming her words succinctly. "Let's go play with them and enjoy the rest of the afternoon."

With that, we both ran to the kids, plucking them off the playset, swinging them around us, and then holding them tightly in a warm embrace.

Then Sheila shouted, "Let's play." All four of us jumped back to the playset as we pushed, carried, and hugged our two little ones for the rest of the afternoon until dinner time.

*****

"I'm getting a little tired. Danny is growing so much he's getting heavier every day." The words were expressed erratically as I breathed heavily. I was carrying Danny in a cloth seat slung over my back and around my shoulders as we hiked up a steep hill on our favorite nature preserve about a twenty-minute drive north of our home.

"Let's sit and rest for a while," Sheila responded to my comment. "Kim, come back here," she commanded loudly while we stopped and sat down. Kim was a very active child and was about twenty yards in front of us. She skipped back to where we sat at hearing Sheila's words.

"Mommy, I want to keep going over the creek. Come on, come on," Kim begged, trying to drag Sheila by the hand.

"Daddy's tired from carrying Danny, so we need to rest for a while. We'll start again soon." Sheila explained to no avail.

"Come on Mommy, come on Daddy. Let's go. Let's go," was the restless response as Kim was skipping around us.

"That's it, darling," Sheila said softly as Kim decided to give in and sit down beside us.

"This is such a great place. So wonderful to walk in the beauty of nature and the unspoiled woods. And, of course, there's the lake we go swimming in on warm days just up the road. I know you have a great time splashing in the water. You can almost swim by yourself." Sheila was trying to occupy Kim while we rested.

"C'mon, let's get started again," I urged, rising slowly from my seated position. Danny was dozing off on my back as Kim bolted to her feet, pulling Sheila with her.

"Wow, you're so strong." Sheila complimented Kim as we returned to negotiating our favorite trail again. Spending an hour or so hiking before Kim tired, we stopped to snack on some trail mix I was carrying before returning to the reserve's parking lot for our drive home.

Arriving home, we ate a quick dinner and then put our two kids to sleep, reading a bedtime story to Kim in her room before she nodded off. Danny had immediately fallen asleep after dinner in his kitchen chair, so we had carried him quietly up to his bedroom and gently placed him in his bed.

"What a great life we've found here," Sheila began when we had returned downstairs, sitting on the couch in our comfortable family room. "The kids are flourishing here, and we both love spending time with them. What with the swimming lake, our hikes in the nature center, playing with our neighbors' kids on the playset. What a wonderful life we have, especially for how we started as two poor kids from Brooklyn struggling to have a family. We are really fortunate everything has turned out so well. This house is so spacious, and with the money you're making, we've been able to furnish it just to our liking."

"It sure is nice to feel like normal parents," I added. "And because of our economic situation, you and I have actually found some time to spend Saturday evenings at some real nice restaurants. I know we were somewhat anxious about hiring a babysitter, but that seems to have worked out quite well. Of course, our weekly routine of every Sunday night at a fast food place with the kids is a lot of fun, and they love it."

*****

"I'm really glad we made the trip out here to enjoy the dinner Sally prepared to welcome us to the area. And Mort seems really nice, too. If he's as good a coworker as he as a host, you must enjoy working with him every day. And what tasty food, and that dessert. Just scrumptious."

"Yeah," I agreed. "Both of them are such genuine people, as was everyone at the dinner."

Leaving Sally and Mort's home, we were walking carefully, slipping and sliding to our car parked just at the curb.

"Damn!" The word came pouring out of my mouth as I wiped my face with my forearm, trying to clear the snow from my eyes. "I didn't realize how hard it's been snowing and for how long. The road is covered, and the darn white stuff is being whipped by the wind, making it almost impossible to see."

"It's a mess. I hope you can clear the snow from the windshield quickly, so we can get going before the roads are impassable. It's a long drive back home," Sheila said.

I opened the car doors and we slid in a bit wet. Then I grabbed a scraper from the back seat and cleared the windshield.

"Not so easy," I remarked as I returned inside the car. "A lot of snow, and it's coming down even harder than a few minutes ago. Good, I put the snow tires on two weeks ago. Start reading the directions to me backwards, and I'll get us going."

Sheila began as usual when we were traveling, but we were skidding all over the road, and the street signs were mostly covered and unreadable, so I followed my nose, trusting my judgment that I could get us back home.

"We need to get back to those kids of ours. We need to make sure they're okay." Sheila was focused only on Kim and Danny as the blizzard intensified even with more fury.

"I'll get us back to them soon," I kept saying. "Real soon." We nearly slid off the road a number of times.

After quite a while, Sheila pointed to our left, saying with some relief, "Look, there's The Clock restaurant on Telegraph Road; now we know where we are. We're getting closer to home. Another twenty minutes in normal weather. Your sense of direction always amazes me, Ken. I don't know how you did it with no visibility and no traction on the road."

"Thanks, babe, but we're not there yet, so let's not celebrate too soon."

"Nonsense, the kids need us home. I hope the babysitter isn't too concerned; we should have been home an hour ago. Kim, Danny, we love you, miss you. Here come your parents," she began to chant. "Daddy will get us home."

We arrived at our house an hour later. Bolting up the stairs, we checked on the kids sleeping in their rooms, kissed them on their foreheads, and returned downstairs. Sheila told our babysitter, Laura, that she would call her parents, informing them that she was to sleep at our house that night, and we'd drive her home in the morning when the storm passed.

"Thanks for your call and your offer. It's nice of you to think of my daughter," Sheila told me Kara responded with sincere appreciation.

Then Kara continued, "Your trip home must have been a nightmare in this driving storm. We've been seeing accident after accident on the news with people stranded in their cars all over the area. This is one of the worst blizzards I've ever seen. How did you guys make it home in one piece?"

Sheila spent the next five minutes responding to Kara, concluding with a warm, "Goodbye, we'll see you sometime tomorrow, Kara."

Then we tried to slow down and relax with a cup of tea in our kitchen as Laura headed upstairs to bed.

"Hey, you know, I guess we really qualify as parents," Sheila stated through a big grin. "In my conversation with the babysitter's mother, she had asked how we made it home through the storm. After I responded, she mentioned it struck her that all I talked about was Kim and Danny, and our need to get home to them. I didn't say anything about the two of us and our drive through the terrible storm. She said it must have been a horrible and very scary trip, yet I didn't say a word about us, about our feelings or experience. Just talked about getting home to the kids.

"I realized that she was right. Through those awful four hours of being pummeled by the storm, sliding all over the road, not knowing exactly where we were, all we could think about was Kim and Danny. Sure, our own safety and wellbeing must have been in the back of our minds, but the kids were first and foremost by far. Just the kids. Our sole focus. We could have been injured or even killed. You know that's how bad it was. But we only could talk about and be concerned about our kids. I think I'm really proud of us," she concluded with a smile. "What do you think?"

"It sounds a bit conceited, but I think I agree. We win the parents award," I joked.

Clanking our teacups together in a congratulatory toast, we chuckled.

*****

"Our life is so full here and complete. Everything is just great," Sheila reflected one Sunday afternoon during the cold, Michigan winter. We were sitting in our family room watching Kim and Danny playing with their toys.

"But sometimes the good feelings are interrupted by recollections and emotions rooted in our past. I can get really sad. It haunts me and gnaws at me.

"The other night when you were gone on your business trip, I was watching television after I put the kids to sleep. A nurse on a news show was demonstrating how mothers whose babies died were allowed to hold the small lifeless bodies in order to say goodbye and get some feeling of closure. Most of the mothers spoke very positively about the experience. As each one spoke, they sobbed. After the second one told her story, I began to cry, a little at first, and then I was crying loudly. I had to stop so I wouldn't wake the kids. That night I cried myself to sleep. I never had the chance to say goodbye to either Carolyn or Matthew. It hurt really bad. I was down for the next two days before you came home.

"And then I think about Jerry's story. That guy who you knew at work. He and his wife were tortured by their circumstances. The needs and heartache of their sick child were all-consuming at the expense of their other two children who they felt they were ignoring. That awful love-hate relationship with that child. They gave up their lives for that kid and still have no hope. I feel for them. We are so much better off. I realize that may sound hard and callous, but we're fortunate to have avoided that type of situation, preventing us from enjoying the life we have. Either Carolyn or Matthew, with just a small change of fate, may have gotten us there, because I know we would love and care for a child like that with all our hearts and energy. We must be thankful we weren't given the choice that Jerry and his wife have to face every day. So thankful.

"Oh, I dislike thinking of those things and getting so down. But I can't help it. It just wells up in me." Her eyes were watery. A tear trickled down her cheek.

"I know. I know," I said, hugging her closely.

CHAPTER 10 -- THE RETURN

"Sit down Ken, please." Sheila requested when I arrived home from work that evening.

I sat without saying a word. Sheila had skipped two menstrual cycles and could not fathom the reason. She had considered some sort of malfunction in her endocrine system as one possibility. The dreaded word, cancer, had also crossed her mind.

Aware of these concerns, signs of worry covered my face, now flushed with anxiety. I was expecting bad news after being told to sit down.

"Oh, I'm so sorry I scared you," Sheila apologized after she noticed my expression. "This is all very mysterious—I'm pregnant!"

"What? But how can that be with the tubal ligation you had?" I questioned her, accompanied by a sigh of relief. Stunned, I nevertheless had a feeling of restrained delight.

"Well, I don't know and neither does the doctor," Sheila explained.

"Is there any chance of a mistake?"

"None at all, the doctor assured me."

I listened as Sheila told me about her trip to the doctor.

"Feels like about two months," the doctor had said as he removed his latex gloves and disappeared from the examination room.

"What?" Sheila said in amazement. The doctor was already out the door and didn't hear her expression of surprise.

"I can't be pregnant. How can I possibly be pregnant?" she'd questioned the doctor when he returned. "I had my tubes tied."

"Well," the doctor began. Sheila said he was a tall, slender man with a confident patrician bearing. He said with a touch of sarcasm, "I've been in practice for over twenty years and perhaps by now I'd know if a woman is pregnant. I could feel the indication of the fetus in the physical exam I just completed. Your vaginal area is distended exactly like any pregnancy of between two and three months. The evidence is unequivocal. You are pregnant, madam. I am absolutely certain. As far as your prior tubal ligation, I cannot elucidate the circumstances around how you became pregnant."

I shook my head in amazement. "You're right. This is very mysterious. On the other hand, it's absolutely wonderful. Don't you think?"

"Yeah, wonderful," she said, flopping on the couch next to me and wrapping her arms around my waist. "Can I kiss you?" she said, frolicking with the good news.

"I can't see why not, madam."

We embraced on the couch, giggling, and clowning around. Infatuated with the possibility of having three children, we were giddy and lightheaded. Our silliness lasted for more than an hour.

After a while, the mood changed as the gravity of the situation set in. We began to seriously discuss our reaction and reached some important life-changing decisions over the next few hours.

"I definitely want to be back in Connecticut so you can deliver at Yale. We can relocate around the greater New Haven area, or somewhere nearby it. I can ask my company for a long-extended leave, which will be awkward. Or I can try to change companies to one located in Connecticut. Then we'll move permanently. Either way, we have to be back where the doctors know us and our history. We need to be where we had success before."

"Sounds pretty drastic and it's a lot to make happen, but I sure agree. The pressure to make it work will be on you, Ken. If anyone can do it, it's you. But you'll also have to walk away from the job you mentioned that the VP talked to you about in Brussels. Remember, it might be a great temporary move and a growth experience for all of us. Learning about Europe and different languages and cultures."

"None of that matters right now," I responded. "We need to be of one focus, and that's getting back to Yale New Haven Hospital."

My career was blossoming. Yet, I knew I would sacrifice my career, the money, and the job gladly if it meant getting back to Yale. We needed to be close to family and friends, our support network. That, plus feeling comfortable with the doctors and the hospital, led us toward our decision.

Sheila's mother told her on the phone that she should consider an abortion. A week before, her sister had made the same suggestion. Sheila had been surprised by the comments but was steadfast in her commitment to see her pregnancy through full-term.

"We can't even consider an abortion given all that Ken and I have been through. I can't accept the concept of ending the possibility of another baby when the both of us have struggled so much in the past to have Kim and Danny. No, I won't have an abortion, and I need your support and Marilyn's support in this decision. I need the two of you not to be fighting me over the next six to seven months. Please, that's what I'm asking you."

Her mother agreed unenthusiastically.

*****

"How can this happen? How can Sheila be pregnant?" I asked Dr. Dawes during our first meeting with him upon our return to Connecticut.

"I thought the doctor in Michigan was loony when he told me," Sheila pointed out. "We're very confused, but of course we are thrilled at the prospects of having another child, especially after our success here with Danny. So, Dr. Dawes, please tell us how this happened?"

"I understand how you feel. Of course, I realize you're confused and trying to discover how something could occur that for you seemed quite impossible. So let me explain in imprecise medical terms, in a way I think that both of you can understand. I'm in no way impugning your intelligence when I say that. In fact, I experience both of you as very bright people. It's just that the procedure is not simple, and I don't want to confuse you even more.

"As adept as we are in obstetrics and surgery here at Yale, unexpected things can happen given the complexity of the human body, especially during situations that deviate from normal. There are, in fact, two existing procedures for a tubal ligation. Given your past history, we chose the less severe procedure because we didn't want to expose you to the incremental risk associated with the more extreme procedure. It simply was not an option. However, when the lower body is distended and stretched well beyond normal as in pregnancy, as the system settles back into its prior shape and proportions, unexpected things can occur."

Sheila and I sat silently, listening intently.

"We believe that as your uterus returned to its regular positioning, one of your tubes may have developed a slight opening or crevice that allowed sperm cells to enter. This is very unusual, to say the least, but it can happen. The odds are extremely long. Of course, I know that you've heard about long odds before."

Dr. Dawes paused for a moment and then said, "I hope that helps."

"To some degree," I responded, "but not completely."

"Yes. I realize that would be the case. Still, I can't provide a better explanation."

"That's fine," Sheila added. "Of course, Ken and I couldn't be happier with the result. It will be a long number of months for us given what we experienced in the past, but we're looking forward to expanding our family. We always wanted more than two kids. And this might be our answer."

"See, that's the good news here. The both of you are excited about your pregnancy, and that's important. Also, you're about half term, and all the tests thus far are quite positive. Right now, you're showing all the trappings of an uninterrupted success. I'm quite confident about a wonderful outcome for you both."

"Thanks, Doctor. We share your enthusiastic optimism. As Sheila said, we're excited about the prospects of having another child. No, not excited, we're ecstatic. But please understand the next few months won't be a cakewalk for us, even anticipating the best result."

"Of course I do. We'll get through this together with flying colors. And if you agree, this time we'll perform the tubal ligation using the more severe method."

With that, Dr. Dawes rose from his large, leather chair and headed out of his office. He stopped on the way to shake our hands.

"Goodbye, I'll see you soon at the next checkup," was all he said, and then left.

Sheila and I followed him out of his office. We walked through the cavernous hospital complex to the multilevel garage where our car was parked. After we drove out on Interstate 95 toward home, Sheila turned to me to share her feelings.

"I'm not sure I'm totally satisfied with the doctor's explanation. Still, since the outcome fulfills our elusive dream for a larger family, I won't quibble with his words. I'm very happy even if I'm not satisfied with the way Dr. Dawes answered our question."

"You and I think so much alike most of the time. I was thinking the same thing you were," I added. "I can only say that the doctor exuded confidence and that made my day."

"Me too."

*****

"Welcome to the company and my department," my new boss said, extending his hand for a hefty shake.

"Thanks. I'm very happy to be here. It feels like home already."

"That's good," he responded. "We're glad to have you. We can really use your analytical skills and expertise in people management. And knowing your personal situation, may I extend you good luck with your wife's pregnancy."

"Thanks."

In short order, I had found a job in Connecticut with a new company. Sheila and I were eager to begin our new life back in the state in which we resided before we relocated to Michigan. With our two kids, we were living in a rental cottage over the summertime until a new house we had contracted to build was completed.

"This is just a great place. Kim and Danny are having a terrific summer spending most of the day at the lake. I like the people I meet. It's all so laid-back here that sometimes I actually forget I'm pregnant. The cloud from our past almost evaporates. I think it was a great idea to rent this place."

"I'm so glad you feel that way," I said. "I'm enjoying it here too. The trip to work every day is a bit too long but coming home and seeing you and the kids enjoying yourselves makes it worth it. And I'm having a ball relaxing at the lake on the weekends.

"And the house is coming along really well. I took a detour tonight from work to see it. The roof is on, and they were installing the wallboard downstairs."

"It's going to be a splendid and spacious place for us to raise our two—oh, oh—I mean three kids." Sheila expanded on my description. "The neighborhood is crawling with other children. Also, it seems to me that you really enjoy your new job. Things are going so great I could scream with joy. But you know, as we've discussed, the past never seems to totally disappear. As confident as I am about this pregnancy, our past experiences haunt me still. I can't help feeling anxious, and just a little scared."

"I know. The past doesn't leave me either. But somehow, this time has an aura of inevitability. The recipe is the same as it was for Daniel. So barring anything unforeseen, it all should work out just fine."

"You're right as usual," Sheila replied.

*****

"Your son has been placed in the Infant Intensive Care Unit as a precaution because of your past experiences. Overall, he's doing fine." Dr. Dawes was standing by Sheila's bed about three hours after Adam, our third child, was born.

"I do need to tell you, though, that he's jaundiced. It's nothing serious right now. Jaundice is not uncommon in infants. It's usually just an indication that the liver is not fully mature, and that usually corrects itself in a few days. We're monitoring his color, which is slightly yellow from the extra bilirubin in his blood. Hopefully, he'll be out of the unit fairly soon and then you'll be able to hold him."

Sheila was crestfallen. Her mouth had been shaped in a large smile in spite of her pain after the C-section. Now, after the doctor spoke to her, an expression of deep concern covered her face. Worry ate at her gut. In spite of her stalwart personality, this development hit her hard, and she was on the verge of breaking down and crying.

"It will be fine," the doctor reassured her, noticing the change in her demeanor.

"You know, Dr. Dawes," Sheila said in a quivering broken voice. "I've heard the words 'normally,' 'usually,' and 'hopefully' before, and because of my history with babies, those descriptions don't give me a great deal of confidence. Being a dental hygienist, I was required to study some amount of pathology in college. I know something about jaundice. It can develop into disease of the liver, and if I remember correctly, can be an indication of blood problems, particularly issues with red blood cells." She paused to gain her composure. "So your news about Adam is not so easy for me to digest. I can't help being very worried and on edge, to say the least."

"Yes, I know your history and your professional background. I'm sorry if I was a bit perfunctory and abrupt in relating the status of your son. I should have spent more time discussing it with you.

"That said, I'm confident Adam has only a mild case of jaundice. His is a temporary situation that will correct itself when his liver stabilizes and begins to function properly. I've seen this many times before in my practice, and I expect your son to make a rapid full recovery. He'll bounce back very soon."

"Thank you, Doctor. And please, there is no need to apologize. It's just that I've been on edge, and anything but the best of news unsettles me."

"I understand completely. Your son is in good hands at the unit. I'm sure you'll be seeing him soon."

Dr. Dawes warmly squeezed Sheila's hand. With a caring smile, he turned to leave her room.

"Don't worry, it'll be just fine," were his parting words.

A few hours later I entered Sheila's room. Smiling, I kissed her on the cheek and wrapped my fingers around her slender arm. Her eyes were wet and red. I could see that she had been crying.

"I've been down with Adam in the Infant Intensive Care Unit and he looks fine." I explained, "They have him under a special light to observe the jaundice. The nurse by his crib assured me that he is improving with every hour and he'll be in your arms soon."

Sheila rubbed her nose with a tissue. Her face lost some of its concern.

"I know. Dr. Dawes was here and told me the same thing. He told me not to worry again. But I'm still upset. Until I can see Adam and hold him, I won't be at peace."

"Sure," I said holding her arm tighter. "It'll be just fine, you'll see."

"Hearing you say you've seen him and he's alright sure helps."

The next morning, I arrived at Sheila's bedside with more good news about our son. He was improving and should be released from the Infant Intensive Care Unit soon, perhaps even that afternoon.

"I just visited Adam a half hour ago and played with his tiny hands and fingers. He looked up at me, and somehow I think he knew I was his father."

"That's wonderful." Sheila laughed with a big grin on her face.

"Oh, that hurts," she said, smarting as she held her hand across her two-day-old incision.

"Ken, come closer, I don't want to talk too loud. The woman in the next bed and I had a long conversation early this morning. She just delivered her fourth baby, and she's quite happy. In the past when she lived in England, she had a baby out of wedlock. Her parents forced her to give the child away. Now, even after having her fourth child, she still mourns the loss of that first baby. We talked and talked for over an hour and we bonded with each other over both of us having lost babies, albeit in different ways."

"That's bittersweet for both of you now that you're in here having children," I reacted.

"Well," Sheila said, "as I laid in bed thinking, after talking to her, I began to develop conflicting reactions, mixed feelings. One was my initial powerful connection with this woman over losing our babies. The other was that without people in a similar situation to hers, we wouldn't have our Kim. There wouldn't be any babies to adopt. I sat in bed for a while and thought about the ironies of life. Bittersweet is right."

Just then a nurse came into the room carrying Adam.

"I know you've been waiting to hold him," the nurse said. "It's not usual for a C-section mother to have her baby so soon after delivery because of some concern over the incision. But Dr. Dawes wanted you to hold your son as soon as possible. So I'm going to slowly lower him into your arms if you fold them across your chest.

Try not to hold too tightly, in order to protect your incision. Okay, are you ready?"

"You bet," Sheila beamed. Her eyes were watery with happiness as she held Adam for the first time.

"Wow, he's so quiet and peaceful. He doesn't kick or fidget." Sheila was in ecstasy holding our third child.

"That's just his personality," the nurse explained. "He was the same way in the Infant Intensive Care Unit."

At that moment we heard some rustling in the hallway.

"Where's the new messiah? Where's the new messiah? Where is he? Oh, he's in room 324." We heard this loud exuberant voice approaching.

"Ah, there he is." A short, dignified-looking man in a lab coat entered Sheila's room. He seemed satisfied that he had found what he was searching for.

"I'm Dr. Feller who assisted Dr. Dawes in your C-section." He was holding a bible in his right hand.

"It says here there will be a new messiah," the doctor explained, holding up the bible so we could see it clearly.

"And this must be him that you're holding. You see when you were on the operating table it was quite clear that nothing was wrong with your tubal ligation. Your fallopian tubes were still tied off and in perfect condition."

"So," he said with a chuckle, "this must be the new messiah. Seriously though, it appeared quite impossible for you to become pregnant. In any event, may I offer you my congratulations?"

The doctor shook my hand as he left the room.

Sheila held Adam for a while, her face beaming. She glowed with the sunshine of a deeply appreciative and happy person. As I gazed at the two of them, I thought that Adam truly was the capstone in our struggle to have a family.

"That was funny, what the doctor said about the new messiah." I broke the silence. "But the part about your tubes still being tied is a bit of a mystery. Seems like a miracle was in the air,"

I said half-seriously.

"Miracle or not," Sheila commented, looking down with loving eyes at the baby in her arms. "He was meant to be."

"All of our children were meant to be."

With her middle finger, she dabbed a tear from her cheek and then lovingly touched my lips with its delicate moisture.

*****

"Come on, Kim. Try to keep up. I know it's a steep hill, but I know you can do it."

Kim heard me from behind the carriage I was pushing, and she stood up on her bike's peddles and passed me like I wasn't even moving.

"Whoa. That was great, Kim, but now slow down so you can ride beside us and your brothers." Sheila talked to Kim in a warm but stern manner. Kim slowed her bike and pulled in close to the carriage, keeping pace with us.

"I am really a mess of sweat," I explained. "Adam is gaining weight every day, so the carriage is heavier. And having Danny riding on the rear axle creates more drag. But I wouldn't have it any other way, the five of us together walking around our new street. It's the best."

"You know it," Sheila chimed in. "Here, let me push for a while now that we're up the hill."

"Hey Danny, hang on, we're making a sharp turn as the street winds over the brook." Danny held on tight to Sheila's knuckles as her hands were tightly wrapped around the carriage handles. I walked and Kim rode close by, completing our wonderful family outing.

"What a great life," Sheila said after we returned to our spacious, newly built custom home. Danny and Kim were playing in the yard with some friends while Adam napped upstairs in his room.

"Things couldn't be better," Sheila continued. "Our new home is just splendid. The neighborhood is great. So many kids. And our neighbors are all mostly new like we are, so everyone is eager to meet one another. It's just a delight.

"Adam is so very easygoing. He's such a good child. Never creates any problems. His only struggle is to keep up with his brother and sister. Kim is so physically gifted and so very beautiful and loving. And Danny. Well, he's so verbally advanced. Remember when the man at the lake was having a long conversation with Danny and told us he had a better chat with Danny than with most adults?" Sheila paused to chuckle as she did every time she told that story.

"I feel the same way," I agreed. "Can't see how things could be any better. And I know how much it means to you to be a critical player in the March of Dimes fundraising and the President of Welcome Wagon. Although sometimes I think you're exhausting yourself, raising the kids, and all of your charity work. I'm glad my mother is coming to visit in a few weeks. I know how much the two of you like each other. And I'm happy that she'll take some of the chores around the kids off your shoulders for a few days. As much as you love it, I know you can use the relief."

"Thanks," Sheila said, "but I couldn't do it all without your help. I love you. You know, Ken," she said, quickly changing the subject, "Sometimes I have thoughts about visiting the unmarked graves where Carolyn and Matthew are buried in New York.

"It used to be a vague, distant, almost undefined feeling rather than a crystal-clear thought. Then, like a puff of mystical smoke, it dissipated. It used to be that way, so I guess that's why I never talked about it. Recently though, the thoughts have become more real and more frequent.

"Something calls me there," Sheila continued, "but I'm torn. After I think it through, I realize we need to leave the past behind and not allow it to distract us from our three kids. We can't let it detract from the joy that Kim, Danny, and Adam bring to our lives. I don't want to carry the darkness of the past to them. We need to keep the bad thoughts from flooding our lives. I think my reluctance to visit the graves is a commitment to the future and a fear of dwelling on the past. I can't allow that misery behind us to consume my thoughts and dreams.

"Although Carolyn and Matthew were with us for only a fleeting moment, they are part of us. We will carry them always. They are expressed in our love, devotion, and nurturing of Kim, Danny, and Adam. So they are part of them, too. They are forever etched in our minds and burned in our hearts. They live on in us and our family, their brothers and sister. I realize we don't need tangible visible reminders. They're in our bodies, our arms, our legs. They are expressed every day in our three darlings. Remembering isn't a physical thing. I will carry them with me forever."

Sheila's face was pensive, expressing sadness and happiness.

"I have similar feelings," I said in a somber tone. "But there's no way I could have expressed them as eloquently as you have. Thanks, that helped me. Maybe we'll go someday, but not now. The time just isn't right."

We sat on the couch holding each other in an embrace of the past and the future.

CHAPTER 11 – EPILOGUE

As the year 2016 came to a close only a few months ago, Sheila and I sat on the couch in our lovely home nestled in the woods. We live in a tranquil quiet Pinelands community in southern New Jersey, complete with a swimming lake and fishing pond, about thirty miles east of Philadelphia.

"We're so very fortunate to live where we do, surrounded by the beauty of nature. Who ever thought that we would wind up in New Jersey, close to where we started, after living all over the country? We learned a lot from spending time on the West Coast, in New England, and the Midwest, meeting people with different views and lifestyles. And we met some of our closest friends in the process. Of course, the best thing about living here by far is being close to our three kids and four grandchildren." Sheila smiled with happiness and gratitude.

"We sure are fortunate," I agreed.

"I have to chuckle when I use the word kids to describe our children. They're not kids anymore. Kim is forty-six, Dan is forty-three, and our baby Adam turned forty-one this year. Do you remember when we called all three of them miracles? Each one really was in their own way."

"Yes, and I still feel that way, given all that happened in the past. I know that you do too."

"And aren't we lucky that Kim married Scott, and Dan married Lisa? It's so wonderful to have them in our lives."

"And our grandchildren." Maddie is almost eighteen, Logan is nearly fifteen, and Gabi and Kass are closing in on twelve. "What a gift they all are."

"The times we spend with them babysitting, at dinners, on birthdays, at soccer games, on holidays and vacations. Those are treasures to be remembered. We'll always cherish them."

"I guess it was all part of the weave of destiny."

ABOUT THE AUTHOR

Ken Lefkowitz earned BA and MS degrees and has pursued business studies at the graduate level. He is currently retired after working as a consultant and senior director for major corporations. His rich experience managing people from all walks of life, various skills and knowledge, and from many locales, was invaluable. A firm believer in women's rights, Ken worked to hire and promote women into professional and supervisory positions at a time when typically, regardless of education or skills, they were relegated to support and secretarial positions. Today, he continues to support women's rights and equality, remaining active in organizations advocating for women's causes. Augmented by the wisdom he acquired as a husband, father, and grandfather, the insight he gained, and his deep understanding of the human condition are reflected in his writing.

www.ingramcontent.com/pod-product-compliance
Lightning Source LLC
Chambersburg PA
CBHW031120080526
44587CB00011B/1054